Praise for

BASE HITS *and* HOME RUN RELATIONSHIPS

"Trina Boice and Coach Cooper have hit it out of the park with this one! This is the all-inclusive, everything-you've-ever-wanted-to-know guide to dating, relationships, and marriage for guys. Laugh, enjoy the baseball jokes and puns, but follow the tips because they'll have women falling for you in no time."

—Rebecca Rode, author of *How to Have Peace When You're Falling to Pieces*

"Using a clever baseball analogy, this book weaves practical ideas and statistics with assignments to help guys understand how to build better relationships with women. The authors use a fun, engaging style to teach critical lessons about a subject that is eternally significant. I highly recommend this book to anyone looking to improve their interactions with others."

—Randal Wright, author of *Make Every Day Meaningful*

"I was having a hard time finding meaningful relationships. Coach Cooper took me under his wing, and we spent an evening going over dating strategies and using them to meet girls. After months of working on and using these strategies, I'm proud to say that I found the meaningful relationship I've been dreaming of and am getting married!"

—Greg G., university student

BASE HITS
and
HOME RUN
RELATIONSHIPS

RELATIONSHIPS

WHAT WOMEN WISH GUYS KNEW

TRINA BOICE
AUTHOR OF THE READY RESOURCE SERIES

CFI
An Imprint of Cedar Fort, Inc.
Springville, Utah

ISBN 13: 978-1-4621-1403-0

Published by CFI, an imprint of Cedar Fort, Inc.
2373 W. 700 S., Springville, UT 84663
Distributed by Cedar Fort, Inc., www.cedarfort.com

Library of Congress cataloging-in-publication data on file.

Cover design by Shawnda T. Craig
Cover design © 2015 Lyle Mortimer
Edited and typeset by Jessica B. Ellingson

Printed in the United States of America

10 9 8 7 6 5 4 3 2 1

Printed on acid-free paper

This book is dedicated to my four wonderful sons: Cooper, Calvin, Bradley, and Bowen. Before I was even married, I knew I was going to have four sons. I saw them in a dream where they were playing in the backyard. They were having a lot of fun and really getting a kick out of each other. I could see that they really loved being together, and I looked forward to the day when I could be with them. They were tall, handsome, happy, and good. I'm so proud to be their mom. I want each of them to have a beautiful and eternal marriage that will be a blessing to them and to our entire family. I pray that this book with inspire them and equip them with the practical tools they need to live happily ever after. I love you guys!

OTHER BOOKS *by* TRINA BOICE

Dad's Night: Fantastic Family Nights in 5 Minutes

Ready Resource for Relief Society volumes 1–4

Sabbath Solutions: More Than 350 Ways You Can Worship on the Lord's Day

Easy Enrichment Ideas: Thinking Outside the Green Gelatin Box

Climbing Family Trees: Whispers in the Leaves

Bright Ideas for Young Women Leaders

Great Ideas for Primary Activity Days

Parties with a Purpose: Exciting Ideas for Ward Activities

Primarily for Cub Scouts

How to Stay UP in a DOWN Economy

103 Creative Ways to Announce Your Pregnancy

A Gift of Love

CONTENTS

ACKNOWLEDGMENTS

Thank you to all of my wonderful friends and family who gave me great ideas to make this book fun and helpful: Tanner Long, Tera and Misha Duncan, Tracey and Larry Long, Brittany and Jordan Olsen, Lori Jones, RJ Bates, John and Susie Bigelow, Vance and Darla Sutherland, Jack and Bette Bates, Ryan Podzikowski, Rachel Heinze, and the wonderful staff at Cedar Fort.

I also want to express thanks to my wonderful editor, Jessica Ellingson, who is always so patient and kind while we work on books together. A big thank-you goes to Kelly Martinez for his marketing expertise and guidance, as well as Emily Chambers for always believing in me.

A huge thank-you goes to my husband, who continually loves me while I try new relationship techniques as our marriage evolves. I will be forever grateful that he found me to be a tolerable companion and continually puts up with my imperfections on my path to improving myself.

Finally, I want to thank my oldest son, Cooper, who has joined me in this writing adventure. I'm so proud of the Christlike man he has become. As a valiant priesthood holder and officer in the

US Army, he is my personal hero; I call him my modern-day Captain Moroni. I think the single guys who read this book will especially appreciate his insights and practical tips on dating and how to understand the female mind.

FOR ALL THE GUYS

Chapter 1

BATTER UP!

THE GAME

In the words of legendary sports announcer Harry Caray, "Hello everybody! It's a bee-yooo-tiful day for baseball!" You've bought this book and stepped up to the plate. That tells me you're really serious about improving your relationship with the woman in your life. Either that or she bought this book for you, and now you have to read it because you *know* she's going to ask you what you learned. Don't worry; it's not going to be that bad. After all, it's partly about baseball, and you love baseball! Romance and baseball are not all that different, actually. They're both skills that you can learn and enjoy for the rest of your life.

You could read an entire book about baseball statistics, but that wouldn't make you a better player out on the field, would it? You have to get out and practice! This book is designed to be read in small sections and put into practice. Read a little bit, and then try an idea or two to see what works for you and your sweetheart. I guarantee you're going to have a ball! (Terrible baseball puns will be included throughout this book in order to keep your eyes rolling and awake.)

Let me first state the obvious that women are different from men. And that's a good thing! A lot of men have a hard time trying to figure out what women want and how they think. It's not that difficult if you learn their language and appreciate the differences. To make it easier, we're going to use terms you might feel comfortable with: the language of baseball.

This book is written for both men who are still in the "minor league" (dating) and men who have been drafted into the "major league" (marriage). *Getting a girl and keeping her are not all that different.* Maybe you've been playing too much baseball and still don't have a woman in your life. This book can help you with that too! This book will help you find a quality woman you can marry and be with for eternity.

This book was conceived one day after my husband and I were discussing our relationship early in our marriage. He's going to get a lot of credit in this book for some of the really great things he does in our marriage. When I need to use him as an example of what *not* to do, I'll just tell you, "I have a friend whose husband . . ." so you'll never know if it's him or really a friend of mine. Hey, I don't want to get in trouble with my husband and end up sitting on the bench.

My husband, Tom, is really creative and has come up with some incredible gifts over the years. Early in our marriage, he really came through on big events such as anniversaries and birthdays, but then there were disappointing and somewhat alarming long dry spells with nothing. No flowers. No romance. *Nada.* Our conversation occurred during one of those dry spells and basically consisted of my pitiful complaints that I was feeling unloved and unappreciated. I suggested that maybe he could replace the few big efforts with more frequent, smaller ones. He thought about that for a few minutes and said, "Oh, it's just like baseball. Home runs are exciting but don't happen that often. It's the small, consistent base hits that win the game." In a baseball peanut shell, that's it!

Paul Richards, Orioles manager, said, "Baseball is made up of very few big and dramatic moments, but rather, it's a beautifully put together pattern of countless little subtleties that finally add up to the big moment, and you have to be well-versed in the game to truly appreciate them."[2] Don't get me wrong, those home runs are wonderful in baseball and in relationships, but it's the small, consistent kindnesses and romantic gestures that keep a relationship going strong on a daily basis.

Ted Williams once said, "Baseball is the only field of endeavor where a man can succeed three times out of ten and be considered a good performer."[3] More often than not, your lady is going to hope for better stats than that when it comes to your relationship.

Take a minute to evaluate all the relationships you've had with women in your life. What did you do right? What did you do wrong that could be improved? Could you tell what worked well and what made you blow it?

Before I started dating, I heard that keeping a good relationship going was a lot of work. I never understood why that could be. I mean, isn't love supposed to be effortless? Well, yes and no. Unconditional love requires nothing. You may be looking for a girl who can cook like your mom, but you're not marrying your mother, who loves you no matter what. Your girlfriend or wife is another creature altogether. If the relationship isn't moving forward, then it's becoming stagnant and stale. Even the best baseball team out there will make some changes each year in the hopes of making it better. To keep the fire going, you have to continue adding some fuel, right? So grab some popcorn, peanuts, and Cracker Jacks and let's play ball!

I'm a mother of four sons, ages fourteen to twenty-six. One of the reasons I wanted to write this book was to help them understand the female mind and prepare them for a successful marriage. When I told them I was working on this book, my oldest son said, "Women talk about what they want, and guys talk about what women *actually* want." He's right. So I invited him to help me write this book for you.

His name is Cooper and he's awesome! (I'm such an unbiased mother.) He's an officer in the army, a BYU graduate, a returned missionary, and an official stud muffin. He's smart, handsome, kind, hilarious, and insightful. He has "field tested" creative dating tips and has learned some really interesting things that he'll share in each chapter's section entitled "Coach Cooper." (We have to stick with the whole baseball theme, you know.) You're going to *love* it. My Coop will give you the scoop on what really works for single guys. Cooper has always been shy, so I want you to know that he has had to work hard at the skills he's going to share with you.

COACH COOPER

First off, I know we're comparing dating to baseball, but I've never liked watching sports. I enjoy being in the ring or on the court, but I've never been interested in watching someone else play, keeping track of stats, or even knowing who's going to the World Series. For me, the only game worth talking about is the game of attraction and dating. I will simply refer to it as The Game because it is the greatest game ever played.

Now, I'm *not* talking about being a player or using mindless tricks to game a girl. I'm going to share some great techniques that will help you find the right girl to spend your life with. Even better, a woman you can share eternity with.

Everyone has played The Game, yet many of us play for a long time without ever knowing the rules, which is ridiculous. If you're like me, you've gone for years not knowing that you didn't know. I was unconsciously incompetent, meaning I just didn't know that I didn't know. After reading this book, you'll be consciously competent!

There are "naturals" out there who are successful, but they usually don't really know why. You probably know someone who has always been successful with women because, well, you're not totally sure. He just is. That's called a natural, but even he needs some of what's in this book. The good news is even though someone can be naturally gifted in any sport, they can be surpassed in *skill* by the average guy who works hard at it and masters the game. The guy who started off with average scores, or even bad ones, is the guy who understands the inner workings of the game much better when he has to work hard at it. He has to go through a lot of pain and push himself to learn things that the natural will never understand.

More good news: like other games, the better you are, the more fun it is, and I promise this is much more rewarding than baseball. I want to help you understand the rules of The Game so you don't make the same mistakes I did.

The principles in this book will take your game to the next level and give you abilities you didn't have before. When one of my brothers started learning The Game and getting good at it, he told me, "I feel like I'm walking around with superpowers." I knew exactly what he meant.

Nothing here is a secret. Men have been using these principles and techniques for years. Like any superpower, it can be used for good or evil. Most of the men in this world who have mastered this material use it to sleep with lots of women. As a member of The Church of Jesus Christ of Latter-day Saints, I expect you to use it for good. You can use it to make people happier, boost their self-esteem, make them laugh, and most important, date and eventually marry a wonderful woman. That's the end goal, and that's how you win the *real* game. Now, good luck, go forth, and win, brother.

STATS

Each chapter will contain some interesting statistics about men and women, dating, and this crazy thing we call love. Enjoy!

- 79 percent of books for men are bought by their wives.
- 87 percent of you will score points with your honey just by having this book on your bedside table. Make sure she sees a bookmark in it so she can tell you're really reading it.
- 23 percent of you reading this book will wonder when it's going to teach you how to improve your baseball swing.
- 42 percent of you will wonder if there's an app for this.
- 64 percent of all statistics are made up.

ASSIGNMENTS

Each chapter will contain some ideas you can put into practice to improve your current relationship or help you figure out how to get one! Even the greatest guy and the best relationship can use some tweaking every now and then. The first-base challenges are to help you ease into The Game. Go for second or third base to up your game. When you're ready to really knock it out of the park, try the home-run assignments.

Now, I'm *not* talking about rounding the bases in the traditional sense the world talks about. I'm referring to bases as increasing efforts and bigger payoff. What I mean is that if you're a beginner in the game of romance or want to start with something easy, then begin with the first-base assignments. They're simple to do, and you'll have some success. If you really want your girl to feel loved and appreciated, go for the home-run assignments. They require more effort, but the payoff is bigger too. "Happy wife, happy life," as people say.

First Base: Set this book out on a table so your girl will see it. Yeah, your buddies will make fun of you. That's okay though; you don't want to kiss your buddies.

Second Base: Put a bookmark somewhere in the book so she'll think you're actually reading it. Be prepared for her to ask you questions about it. Let her know it is the most fantastic book ever written.

Third Base: Read the doggone book already!

Home Run: Read the book *with* your girl. Ask her questions. Talk about it.

A LEAGUE OF THEIR OWN

This is a section that will be at the end of each chapter just for the ladies. Girls, you're not off the hook here. *You* have work to do too. A happy, healthy relationship includes two people.

A friend of mine was recently divorced, and I asked him what advice he thought I should share with you in this book. He believed he had a happy marriage for almost twenty-five years. One day, his wife announced she wanted a divorce. He was shocked and admitted that he had never seen it coming. He said to me, "It takes two people to build a successful relationship, but only one to destroy it."

Now, I'm sure he wasn't completely guiltless. No one is ever 100 percent to blame when a relationship fails. The sad thing is that she never told him why she wanted out of their marriage. To this day, he still doesn't know. He told me it's really hard to know what to work on and improve when he doesn't know what he's doing wrong. Now, he may have been so self-absorbed that he didn't pay attention to the signs, but his wife expected him to be able to read her mind. We girls tend to do that, and it's not fair to our men. Cut them some slack. Men and women really do think differently, so how could he possibly know what you're thinking or how you feel at every moment? Sometimes, *we* don't know why we feel the way we do ourselves, so how on earth is he supposed to know?

If you have a good guy (I'm assuming you do because he's actually willing to read this book), then know he *wants* to make you happy. He just needs to learn *how*. Every female he's ever known has a different set of instructions. Be patient and help him know what his actions mean to you. Then ask *him* how he sees the ideal girlfriend or wife. The most important thing is to get the conversation going.

So ladies, *your* homework is to write down a list of ten things your man does right. You fell in love with him for a reason. Don't let that sink full of dirty dishes make you forget why.

Chapter 2

THE RULES OF ROMANCE AND LOVE LANGUAGE

The rules of The Game in your relationship will depend a lot on your woman. There are some basic standard-issue rules, such as never forget her birthday or your anniversary, never leave the toilet seat up, and never regift jewelry that your ex-girlfriend returned to you after you broke up. However, a lot of rules will be determined by what is important to her.

Unfortunately, there isn't one model of woman with only one instruction manual. For example, does your girl want you to open the door for her as a grand gesture of chivalry or would she rather do it herself to assert her feminine strength and independence? Do a dozen red roses tell her you love her or would she rather have a single daisy from your backyard? Now, you may not see the difference (though the daisy sure costs a lot less), but she sees the small subtleties and may hear a distinct message. If you want her to hear what you're really saying, you need to know what language she speaks.

There has been a lot of talk about "love language" in the last couple decades or so, and I think it's extremely important to the success of any relationship. I highly recommend the book *The 5 Love Languages* by Gary Chapman. Love language simply means that people interpret actions or words differently and assign meaning to them based on their experiences and values. Find out what your girl's love language is. Does she feel loved when you buy her gifts, spend time with her, or have long talks? Maybe she "hears" your love when you do acts of service for her or you actually tell her those three magical words out loud ("I love you"). Ask her what actions you could do that would tell her she is loved by you. On the flip side, find out what kinds of behavior would send her the message that she's not important to you or that you just don't care.

Simply asking her what she likes is a good first step. Be genuine and she'll be flattered and eager to teach you.

Now, you may get a girl who is insulted by your question and says something like, "Well, if you don't know, then there's no hope for us!" Yes, she's being dramatic, but her reaction may just be to test your sincerity. If she hasn't read the first chapter, then she may be unfairly expecting you to read her mind. She'll think you don't love her if you can't tell what she's thinking. Ask again, explaining that you want to make sure to get it right and you truly want to please her. If she sees that you really mean it, she'll soften and open up her heart. Some women simply don't know how to tell her man what she wants. Encourage her to be specific.

When my husband and I were first married, I began our new life together by doing all of the things that I thought were supposed to be done by the perfect wife (based mostly on what I saw my parents do or read in books or even observed on TV and in movies). I baked cookies and gourmet meals and fussed over little things around the house. When I wasn't getting the grateful reaction from an adoring husband I thought I was supposed to get, I decided to find out what he *really* wanted in a wife. He didn't want all of the sweets in the house to tempt his waistline and he said he'd rather have a simple meal if that meant I was in the kitchen less and with him more. What a revelation! We decided to write a list of what we both thought the perfect spouse was, and we were equally surprised at how differently we had ranked various efforts.

Find out how your woman "hears" love. Does she hear the words "I love you" when you bring her flowers or chocolates when it's not a special occasion? Or do those words ring loud and clear when you volunteer to wash the dishes or do a load of laundry? (Hint: most women *really* want help with the housework.) You may think you're supposed to buy an expensive gift for her on Valentine's Day (mostly because the ads on the radio tell you so), but maybe what she really wants is an hour of your undivided attention or a handmade card that features your wit and charm . On second thought, you'd better show up with at least one flower just in case or you could end up sitting in the dugout. Flowers and a card really are the bare minimum on Valentine's Day. That's your heads-up.

You may think it's silly to sit, hold hands, and stare into the fireplace (especially when there's a great ball game on TV), but to her, that may mean everything in the world. So one of the first "cardinal" rules of a successful relationship with a woman is to find out what's important to her.

Now here's the deal, guys, and this is big: It doesn't matter so much what you say or what your actions are, but it's how she *interprets* those words or actions that will determine whether you've hit a home run or struck out in the game of love. It's all about expectations.

I suppose I could end the book with those last two sentences. Keep reading anyway. You and your girl come from different backgrounds and life experiences, so your expectations are probably different. Find out what she hopes to get out of a relationship and what she expects her man to be and do. Write it down. Here's the tricky part: she may not be able to readily identify what she needs. She'll start telling you about her wants first. As she matures in love and life, she'll learn what it is she really needs. Get an eraser.

What may be important to her last year may not necessarily be important to her in ten years. *What?* Yep, it's true. A woman is ever changing, and yes, her fluctuating hormones have something to do with it. It may not be rational either. Welcome to the confusing world of estrogen. Just appreciate the evolving creature in front of you. They say women have cleaner minds than men; that's mostly because they change them so often.

"What about us single guys?" you ask. The lesson in this chapter is all important when trying to woo a new girl. Find out what she likes. All those slick moves that worked on your last girlfriend might not work on the new girl.

Get all the main stats on your girl. These will come in handy when you're trying to come up with a special gift or act of service that she'll love. (Think home run.) Ask her what her favorites are:

- Color
- Dessert
- Flower
- Ice cream flavor
- Fruit
- TV show
- Movie
- Superhero
- Scripture
- Quote
- Holiday
- Website
- Magazine
- Musician
- Celebrity
- Dinner
- Song
- Cereal

- Restaurant
- Cartoon character

Women want romance, but what they really want is to be understood and supported in the things they value most. Read that sentence again, guys.

COACH COOPER

You're about to get a lot of advice on playing The Game. The point isn't to become clever and manipulative; it's to become a better man. By becoming a better, more attractive man, women will start coming to you and you'll find that your reality changes. Instead of living in a world of limits where you choose between only one or two girls who are willing go out with you, you'll have a world of choices and options. You'll be able to date just about anyone.

Before I teach you to play The Game, I want you to remember this: use the least amount of game possible. If you start talking to a girl, sparks fly, and you two instantly connect without using any cool techniques, that's great! However, in *my* experience, every girl is affected by The Game (even the girls that say they don't like The Game) because a lot of it is simple psychological reality.

Another quick bit of advice: while on this journey to find (and attract) the woman of your dreams, have fun. If you're not having fun, you're doing something wrong. If you are having fun, women will notice, and they like that.

STATS

- "Couples usually wait until six to eight dates before they are willing to enter into an exclusive relationship."[6]
- "Speed-dating was invented by a rabbi from Los Angeles in 1999, and is based on a Jewish tradition of chaperoned gatherings of young Jewish singles."[7]
- "The most common time for breakups is around three to five months."[8]
- On free dating sites, about 10 percent of new accounts are scams.[9]

ASSIGNMENTS

First Base: Write a list of qualities you want in a woman.

Second Base: Ask your girl for a list of qualities she wants in a man.

Third Base: Compare lists and see what you can do to acquire the qualities on her list.

Home Run: Write a list of all the great qualities your woman already has. Share one item with her each day by writing it on a notecard and attaching it to a flower. Do one each day for a week or an entire month. She'll love the accumulated bouquet of flowers, but she'll really love that you see who she is.

A LEAGUE OF THEIR OWN

Okay, girls, ask your guy the same questions above to find out his favorites. Here are a few more categories you could ask him about:

- Sports team
- T-shirt
- Season
- Historical hero
- Board game
- Tongue-twister
- Joke
- Sandwich
- Mobile app
- Video

Chapter 3

THE BALLPARK

WHERE THE GAME IS PLAYED: HEAD AND HEART

The ball game is played in the ballpark. The game of love is played in the head and heart. Men and women really do think differently. To be honest, girls think guys are knuckleheads sometimes. It's only because they don't understand how guys think any more than guys understand girls.

Here are a few examples. Realize, of course, these are generalizations.

Men can compartmentalize. Women see the whole picture. That's why you ask yourself if the date went well at the end of the night and she has already named your third child.

Men can focus on a single tree, or the task at hand. Women become distracted by the forest, making them unable to recognize the tree in front of them. That's one reason why men can hang Christmas lights and why women can't back their cars into a parking stall.

Men think rationally. Women think emotionally. That's why you pick out the cheapest birthday card at the store in two minutes and she spends twenty minutes analyzing every nuance of how the receiver will interpret the card's message.

Men can turn off their brains. Women can't. That's why men can go fishing for hours and women will worry about whether the teal napkins at your wedding will coordinate with the salmon on the plate next to the calla lilies in the centerpiece on the table, especially if Aunt Paula is sitting next to Cousin Brittany, who recently returned from her mission to Japan where she . . .

Men enjoy the moment. Women often can't enjoy the present because of what might happen in the future. That's why men can take a nap on the expensive designer pillows on the couch and women can only see how much it's going to cost to have them dry-cleaned if dirt or drool get on them.

Men are generally more satisfied with themselves. Women are not. That's why a woman won't believe you when you tell her she's the prettiest thing you've ever seen.

Men don't notice details as well as women. That's why you can happily drive your dirty pick-up truck around town and all she sees are the water bottles and hamburger wrappers scattered on the seats.

Men want to go from point A to point B. Women want to experience the journey. That's why men's sentences are short and women's conversations last for hours.

Men don't have curves. Women do. That's why you want them.

Men have testosterone. Women have estrogen. That's why men want to get frisky and women want to rock babies.

Isn't it wonderful that Heavenly Father created us with all of our perfect flaws and differences? Wouldn't life be boring if we were the same? We certainly wouldn't be attracted to each other if we were. Together, we complete each other. Pretty brilliant, right?

If everyday items were designated as male or female, they would further illustrate our funny differences.

- Freezer bags: They are male because they hold everything in, but you can see right through them.
- Photocopiers: They are female because once turned off, it takes a while to warm them up again. They are effective reproductive devices if the right buttons are pushed, but they can also wreak havoc if you push the wrong buttons.
- Tires: They are male because they go bald easily and are often overinflated.
- Hot air balloons: They are male because to get them to go anywhere, you have to light a fire under them.
- Sponges: They are female because they are soft and squeezable and retain water.
- Web pages: They are female because they're constantly being looked at and frequently getting hit on.
- Trains: They are definitely male because they always use the same old lines for picking up people.
- Egg timers: They are female because, over time, all the weight shifts to the bottom.
- Hammers: They are male because they've hardly changed at all in the last five thousand years and they are handy to have around.
- Remote controls: They are female. You probably thought it would be male, but consider this: he'd be lost without it and while he doesn't always understand how it works, he keeps trying.

Married guys, you've probably discovered some of these frustrating differences by now. Enjoy them. Love them. Laugh at them. Live with them.

Single guys, now is the time to make the decision about the kind of person you want to spend the rest of your life with while your head is clear. When you're in love, your heart and your hormones can easily take over your brain. It's a fact. There are certain decisions you can make right now, and later you can fill in more details as you gain experience with different kinds of personalities and choices. You're in the "gathering information" stage.

Don't get fixated on one kind of person or hair color. For example, date athletes *and* nerds, blondes *and* brunettes. Just like when you go out to eat at a restaurant, try lots of different things on the menu. You might even be surprised at which one fits better than you had originally thought.

When I was single, I had two lists of qualities to help me determine the guy I wanted to marry:

- *Has* to be
- Would be nice to be

The items on my first list were non-negotiable. The second list had things I was looking for in a guy, but they weren't deal breakers.

Now remember, it's far more important to develop your own qualities than to just create a shopping list for what you want in a future wife. Do you possess the qualities you're looking for in a wife? Marriage is not so much *finding* the right person as it is *being* the right person.

When I was in college, I was completely in love with this one guy and could seriously see myself marrying him. He even had *all* the qualities on my "would be nice to have" list. He was perfect. After dating for many months, I started noticing some red flags that made me realize he was missing one important quality: integrity. No biggie, right? Wrong.

I simply didn't feel like I could trust the guy. How are you supposed to trust your life and your eternity in the hands of someone who isn't completely honest? A lack of integrity is a red flag indicating thay someone has the potential to have an affair after you're married. I really worried about that because too many marriages had ended due to infidelity that affected my life in some way. Girls worry that a guy who is dishonest in business could cause their future family to fall into financial ruin. Someone who isn't true to the Lord could become less active or even leave the Church. I realized that this one simple quality was a big deal breaker for me. Integrity suddenly jumped to the top of my list of "has to be." Girls will analyze every aspect of your character when dating.

Those first impressions count, but you'll need to dig deeper to discover what someone is really like. That's what dating is for. While you're busy making your lists and looking for that perfect person, remember that you should be developing those qualities yourself because they're probably on your future spouse's list too.

Make these decisions right now and keep your commitments. Write down what you will and will not accept:

- My future spouse will be
- My future spouse would never

- My future spouse always
- My future spouse has
- My future spouse does
- My future spouse can't
- My future spouse is

You need to date different kinds of people before you can intelligently make the best choice for a marriage partner.

COACH COOPER

If you want to master The Game, what should you work on first? That depends on where you're weakest. Professional baseball players know that the first step to success is conquering your own head. You can't play The Game well until you can control what's in your own head and heart.

If you're incredibly shy, work on that. If you're overweight, work on that. If you don't do anything exciting, work on that. And don't fall for one of the biggest lies ever told: "I can't change." The enemy has been telling people this lie since the beginning of time, and he knows he's succeeded if he can get you to say it to yourself. It's the most diabolical lie ever!

You can do anything you set your mind to. You can change almost any aspect of your life, and I only say "almost" because you can't train yourself to see through walls or fly. Well, at least not in this life. You can change your personality. You can change what you look like. You can change the way you talk. You can change the way you carry yourself. You can change your social network. I'm serious. That's why we're here. And I'm not talking about change in a bad way. You should change yourself. I'm not trying to tell you not to be you anymore. That's impossible. What I'm saying is to become a better you. Life is about progressing. Become the *you* that you really want to be.

The ballpark is where the game is played, and that starts with *your* head and heart.

STATS

- "In a survey conducted by MSNBC.com and *Elle* Magazine, more than 31% of men said they had dumped an overweight partner, compared to 12% of women who had done the same thing."[12]
- "Women who post a photo on Internet dating sites receive twice as many email messages as women who don't."[13]

- "On internet dating sites, men who reported incomes higher than $250,000 received 156 percent more email than those who earned only $50,000."[14]
- If a man can't decide what to wear on a date, he should probably choose blue. "Studies show that women are attracted to men in blue."[15]
- "Thirty-three percent of online daters form a relationship, 33% do not, and 33% give up."[16]

ASSIGNMENTS

First Base: Finish filling out those lists. Yeah, I know you didn't really do them when you read it the first time.

Second Base: Talk to a girl you don't know.

Third Base: Ask out a girl whom you think isn't normally your type.

Home Run: Ask out a girl whom you think is out of your league.

A LEAGUE OF THEIR OWN

Girlfriends and wives, encourage him to have "guys' night." Get to know his friends and support his need to have bros. Men and women *are* different. Understand and celebrate his differences.

So he wants to play video games or watch baseball on TV? An hour or two isn't going to kill you. Don't be so needy. Would you really rather have him looking up cute crafts and fancy recipes for you on Pinterest? That's what girlfriends are for. Let him be a man.

Now girls, if he's playing video games for hours on end all of the time, then you really don't have a man, do you? Nope. What you have on your hands is a ten-year-old boy in a man's body and a problem. Move on.

Wives, create some kind of a "man cave" where your husband can be a guy without all of your lace and potpourri. You want to live with a man, not just a roommate, right? Work on developing the qualities that make you a great person, not just a great catch.

Chapter 4

HEAVY HITTER

BE. A. MAN.

Be. A. Man. You're the man. You take the lead. Be a man and you'll make her feel like a woman. Women don't like dictators, tyrants, and despots, but they respect a strong leader. Women want a strong male figure at the head of the house. They want to have a strong shoulder they can lean on when they're weary. They don't want to see you scream when you see a spider. You're the man; you're the one that's supposed to be her hero and kill it. I know she's probably capable of killing that spider, but she asked you to do it so she can adore your heroism.

In baseball, the team has to have a leader, whether it's the manager or the coach. There would be chaos if all the players just did whatever they felt was best. The players trust the leader for his expertise and judgment.

Most women want the man to lead and be the knight in shining armor. She also wants you to make her feel like a woman. Grab her. Kiss her. Make the move. Dip her. Kiss her again. Hold her hand. Put your arm around her. (Yes, this applies to you old married folks. Make her feel young and sexy again.)

Women *want* to admire their men. They want a hero. They want to feel safe in your arms. They want to be protected. They want to feel lucky they were able to catch your eye and be chosen by you. They want to be proud of you. They want to brag about you to their friends. They really do want you to take the lead.

If you're married, take the lead as the priesthood holder in your home. Organize family home evening and temple trips. Those are not "women's work." Make sure your family is prepared for emergencies and is doing service for others. Your wife most likely took *your* last name when she married you, so don't expect her to be in charge of genealogy. The family proclamation states that *you* are to provide and protect.[18] Honor your priesthood and she will eagerly follow you to the ends of the earth. Be a godly man and she will want to join you in eternity.

Have a plan for a date, whether you're single or married. Don't just ask, "What do you want to do?" She'll most likely say, "I don't know. What do *you* want to do?" Sometimes she *will* care. If so, do that. Sometimes she wants to see how creative you are or how much you care. Sometimes she's just exhausted and wants you to take the lead. Sure, you can take turns later, but in the beginning, *you* be the one to make it happen.

That being said, she also wants to be your equal partner in the decision-making. I know it seems like a paradox. Work with me here. Counsel with her. You're not her boss. Listen to her. She may actually point out some things you didn't notice. Together, you can be a powerful team for good. God created Adam *and* Eve. Only *together* are you complete.

COACH COOPER

My Journey: The Story of an AFC (Average Frustrated Chump)

I'm not all about telling life stories. But I'll tell you a part of my life story that has to do with dating. Why do you care? You don't.

Unless it's similar to your story, in which case it could change your life.

I won't start at the beginning of my story. I'll start at the end of one story and the beginning of another. The first story stinks, but the one that came after was awesome.

"I think you might just be more into me than I'm into you." These were words coming from a girl I had dated for almost a year. "Why can't you just have better game? I want to be more into you. I really do."

I'm not kidding. That conversation really happened. She told me I didn't have enough game, and after a year of dating the girl of my dreams, it ended. She was sweet, smart, beautiful, funny, and everything I wanted. She told me that I was the perfect guy and that there was nothing I could do or change to be better. She just couldn't see us being together any longer. The funny thing is that the girl I had dated before her told me the exact same thing.

This isn't a sob story. It's a story of success! Thanks to that moment, my life completely changed. I was so frustrated and annoyed with women that I determined I would do whatever it took to figure them out. And I did. I discovered the "pickup community," a community of men dedicated to helping each other learn the secrets of attracting women.

My problem was the same as every other average frustrated chump (AFC). I didn't know what I was doing, and I caught a bad case of "one-itis," a condition common to AFCs. I thought this girl was "the one" and I put her up on a pedestal. I lived to make her happy, and everything I did was an attempt to win her over. In my mind, she was perfect, special, and different from all the other girls. I would go out of my way to cater to her needs and do whatever she wanted to do.

Of course, I got dumped. I would have dumped me too. The problem was I didn't know how to be a man! Every girl loves to be chased, but subconsciously they all want the guy they can't have.

If you've ever had one-itis and lost her, the best thing you can do is forget about her and start dating other women. You quickly realize there is a sea of women out there who are just as good as or better than the one you were hung up on.

President Kimball said, "'Soul mates' are fiction and an illusion; and while every young man and young woman will seek with all diligence and prayerfulness to find a mate with whom life can be most compatible and beautiful, yet it is certain that almost any good man and any good woman can have happiness and a successful marriage if both are willing to pay the price."[19]

With that figured out, I set out on a journey. I took in a lot of material about picking up and attracting women and finally realized what I was doing wrong, as well as what I was doing right. At one point in the journey, I even did a thirty-day challenge to implement something new into my game each day. The goal for the challenge was to have a date by the end of the thirty days, but a girl actually asked me out on day four. I had known her for years, but all of the sudden she was into me? A whole new world was opening up. After a few months, this was happening more and more. One week, I was asked out by five different girls. I used to think that girls never asked guys out. Apparently I was wrong.

I learned how to flirt, banter, and play games. I learned the principles of preselection and disqualification. I wasn't as shy anymore, and I found out that girls actually wanted me to make decisions. I could go on a date every night of the week and multiple times in the same day, if I had the time. I was getting phone numbers from girls I never intended to call, just because it was a challenge and I wanted more practice.

My life story as an AFC came to a close and a new story began. My wish is for every AFC out there to see what I saw: a world filled with opportunity and women. Lots of cute women. Now, I'm not God's gift to women. I'm just a regular guy who learned a thing or two about playing The Game and it changed my life. Keep reading, because I'm going to share with you what I learned in the following chapters.

STATS

- The third week in September is National Singles Week in the United States.[20]
- "According to the US census, there are 95.9 million unmarried people in the United States, of which 47% are men and 53% are women."[21]
- "Researchers at the University of Chicago found that people were twice as likely to find a date through friends and family than through the bar scene."[22]
- "Psychologists at the University of Pennsylvania studied data from over 10,000 speed daters and found that most people make a decision regarding a person's attraction within three seconds of meeting."[23]

ASSIGNMENTS

First Base: Ask her out on a date and have a plan.

Second Base: Be creative in your invitation to go on a date.

Third Base: Open her doors, bring her flowers, and make her feel feminine.

Home Run: Do a kind act of service for her, like taking out the trash or doing the dishes. Home runs can be simple, yet they show love and appreciation in a big way.

A LEAGUE OF THEIR OWN

Let him be a man. Women today are extremely independent. That's great, but it can also be a problem in male-female relationships. You want to feel needed, right? Well, so does your man. Yes, you're perfectly capable of bringing home the bacon *and* frying it up in the pan, but let him know he's you're hero when *he* does those things.

If a man has an affair, it's usually because he likes how the new girl makes him feel. A wife expects and demands; the new woman acts delighted about everything he says or does. You did that once too.

When you point out all of the things he doesn't do well, he feels like less of a man. Why would he want to be with someone who does that to him? Instead, make him feel like your hero. You've heard of a nagging wife, right? Girls, don't be one of those. Constantly complaining and whining about every little thing will cause your husband to fall out of love faster than almost anything else.

A man's ego is a delicate thing. Women most want to feel loved and understood. Men want to feel admired and respected by their women. There's nothing wrong with that. That's one way men and women are different. Accept it and honor it.

FOR SINGLE GUYS

Chapter 5

OPENING DAY

FIRST IMPRESSIONS

As they say, you only have one chance to make a first impression. Chapter 9 will give you more details on how you should dress and smell, so for this chapter, let's just say you have those bases covered and you're now working on confidence. Girls don't like cocky "playas," but they *are* attracted to humble confidence. Yeah, all you guys are probably rolling your eyes now because you've lost a girl to some handsome jerk.

Here's the deal, just go up to a girl and start talking. I know it's super scary. Do it anyway. Be brave or be single! Cooper will give you a ton of ideas on how to do it in a minute. What kinds of guys get the beautiful girl in the end?

- Rich guys
- Brave guys

If you've served a full-time mission for the Church, then you've experienced rejection and know it's a bit of a numbers game. Dating girls is kind of the same thing. You *will* be rejected. Just count on it. Once a girl shuts you down, look at it as one rejection closer to the yes that will inevitably come.

Dating should be fun and casual. That being said, you marry whom you date, so dating is also serious business. Use it as a tool to learn more about the person you're dating and whether she is a right match for you in marriage. The first date can set the tone for an entire relationship and determine whether a second date happens at all.

How do you start a conversation anyway? It's easy; just open your mouth. Seriously, it's not as hard as it seems. Walk up to someone cute and say:

- You're really good at your calling. How long have you had it?
- You look like someone who likes fun. Have you ever watched BYU's Studio C?
- I've never seen you at school/church/work before. Are you new here?
- Did you see that guy with the green Mohawk today? (You'll always score points with her when you make her laugh.)

Here's the trick: ask questions. People are flattered when they think someone is genuinely interested in them. Here are some more examples:

- What did you think of that meeting/announcement/class/TV show today?
- My sister would love that jacket you're wearing. Where did you find it?
- I heard there's a singles' activity going on next weekend. Do you know anything about it?

Don't ask yes-no questions, but rather open-ended ones that get the other person thinking and talking. Here are even more examples:

- I noticed you were reading that book. What is it about?
- I noticed your cool cell phone because I'm thinking about switching. What features do you like about it?
- I'm doing a survey about popular mobile apps. Which ones do you like the best?

Everyone likes to laugh, so if you can start a conversation with something funny, even better. The first time my husband called me on the phone (after we had met in person), he asked, "So, do you know how to get a pot pie out of the cardboard holder without breaking it?" It made me laugh and feel like I was rescuing a helpless bachelor.

If delivered with a playful smile, some of these funny pickup lines might actually work. Be careful, however, or you'll just come off as a creepy stalker.

- Do you want to carpool to the celestial kingdom?
- I've got to be honest with you. I'm a tool . . . in the hands of the Lord.
- Are you a search engine? Because you've got everything I'm searching for.
- Do you want to sit with me in church . . . forever?

I always tell my sons to boldly go up to the most gorgeous girl on campus and say, "My mom wants me to date someone beautiful so that she has good-looking grandchildren." For some reason, though, they just can't bring themselves to say that.

COACH COOPER

OPENERS

Opening is often one of the most difficult parts of The Game. Why? Because it makes us nervous. There are a lot of different trains of thought on how to get over approach anxiety (called AA by some), but in my opinion, giving this state of fear a name like "approach anxiety" is like creating a disease out of a natural condition that everyone has. Everyone gets a little nervous approaching a beautiful woman. Even when you're a master of The Game, the fear is still there. You just have to know how to deal with it. It's completely normal, and the cure is to man up and go talk to her. You can do whatever you like to get pumped up and motivate yourself, but in the end, either you man up and talk to her or you end up like the other guys who are too scared and you go home with regrets at the end of the day.

A great example I've heard is that approaching women is like jumping into a pool. You're always a little hesitant before you jump in because you know the water's cold. Once you jump in, you get used to it, and it's easy to jump in again and again. The next day, however, it doesn't matter that you were used to it the day before. Now you're warm, dry, and just as nervous about jumping in again. So it is with approaching a girl. The first approach of the day is always the hardest, but once you conquer your fear and do it, any approach after that is much easier. Don't worry, after weeks or months of jumping in, your fears slowly disappear to the point that you won't think twice about it anymore.

DIRECT OPENERS

Walking up to a girl and telling her you think she's beautiful works better in some situations than in others. If you're going to compliment a beautiful woman at a social event, you should mention something other than her appearance. For example, "I noticed you look people in the eyes when you talk to them. Hardly anyone does that around here, and I think it's pretty cool." A genuine compliment about her personality will knock her socks off. Even if you get shut down, you will feel like you're the man for having the courage to go up to a gorgeous girl and introduce yourself.

If you're just walking down the street, it's perfectly fine to stop a girl and talk to her. Women love being approached by confident men. You never know when a girl has had a bad day or is already in a relationship, but they will almost always be completely flattered and surprised by your confidence. If she's single, you will be well on your way to getting her number and setting up a date.

In fact, when you realize how easy this is, it might blow your mind. How often have you walked past a beautiful girl and thought to yourself, "If only there were some way to meet her." Well, guess what? The world is yours and you can go up to and meet anyone you'd like! All you have to do is stop the girl you were about to walk past and say, "Hey, I thought you were cute, and I had to meet you. I'm (insert name here)."

You will almost always get a positive response, and if she doesn't have a boyfriend, you can easily ask for her phone number after talking for a few minutes. The essential element of this approach is confidence. That's it. It doesn't matter what you say. It doesn't matter what you look like. There is a group of guys who film themselves approaching girls like this and they create different challenges just to make it harder, like being in a wheelchair, wearing a fat suit, or having food on their faces. No matter what they do, they usually get phone numbers because they're confident and honest about what they want.

This is what direct openers are all about: being confident and telling a woman you're interested. Direct openers are great for when you're walking down the street, at the grocery store, at a bookstore, or jogging. You're probably not going to run into these women again, so you really have nothing to lose. If you try to start up a conversation by asking for directions, it'll look like you're interested in them but don't have the guts to come out and say it. Instead, be bold and have fun with it. I'll be the first to admit that it's difficult to walk up to a girl and say she's cute, but it's just like jumping in the pool.

My brother and I once put together a list of cheesy "Mormon pickup lines" and used them on girls around campus at BYU and BYU–I. It was partly for fun, but also to prove that it doesn't matter what you say as long as you're confident and having fun. I recommend something simple like, "Hey, I thought you were cute so I wanted to meet you."

Make it playful. A great game you can play is called "Go." The rules are simple. You go out with a friend or several friends and when you see a cute girl, you point to her and tell your friend, "Go!" He has to go talk to her, no matter what, even if she's on her phone, working in a store, or whatever. If he can get a phone number, great; if not, he gets respect for trying. If your friend chickens out and fails to approach her, he has to do ten pushups on the spot. Ideally, you're in a crowded place so there are lots of girls, and it's embarrassing to start doing pushups when there are people everywhere.

One of two things happens: either you start approaching girls right away or you chicken out and end up doing pushups in a public place. Once you've done a few sets of pushups, the anxiety disappears because you realize you already look like an idiot. It then becomes way easier to approach a good-looking girl because you don't care about being embarrassed anymore.

INDIRECT OPENERS

An indirect opener is, well, less direct. It allows you to slip onto the field without projecting interest in a girl the second you meet her. It could be a preplanned opinion opener such as:

- "I've only got a minute, but I need a female opinion on something. My friend over there and I have been arguing over what makes a movie a chick flick. There's some kind of romance in almost every movie, so how do you decide if it's a chick flick or not?"
- "Hey, let me get your opinion on something, and then I need to get back to my friends. Mustaches: yes or no? I'm trying to convince my buddies to grow out mustaches for a trip we're going on, but they're worried they won't be able to get a date with a one. What do you think?"

Notice in the two examples above, both questions are preceded by a time constraint, which is meant to put the girls at ease. Otherwise, they'll have the thought that they might be dealing with a weird guy they can't get rid of.

Time constraints give a reason why you can't stay for long. It takes the pressure off and stops a girl from thinking, "How long is this guy going to be here?" It changes her mindset from "What if he doesn't go away?" to "How can I get him to stay?"

Opinion openers are old school, but if you can't think of another way to approach, why not? Just keep in mind that all it does is get you talking to her. At the end of the day, she doesn't really care what you talked about. She cares about how she felt while the two of you were talking.

SITUATIONAL OPENER

Instead of using something canned, you're going off an observation to start a conversation. Examples include:

- "Hey, did you see the guy with the unicycle outside?"
- "I've never been here before. What's the deal with the giant moose head on the wall?"

I'll reiterate this because it's so important. A hundred men could say the exact same thing to a woman and she would have a different reaction each time. What really matters is how you make her feel. That's what she'll remember. Your confidence, vibe, posture, and tone of voice all matter more than what you say, to a large extent.

STATS

- Depending on the type of woman a man would like to meet, he should visit that type of clothing store. For example, if a man likes outdoorsy women, he should go to an outdoor clothing store to meet women.
- If a group of women are standing together, but their eyes are wandering, they are likely looking for guys to meet. If they each take a turn to break away from the group, they are probably making themselves available so men can approach them.
- A woman who is interested in her date will express it in ways she may not even realize: laugh at his jokes, play with her hair,

fidget with an object, blush, pucker her mouth, stumble over her words, or lean in toward him.

ASSIGNMENTS

First Base: Walk up to any female at church, smile, and say hi.

Second Base: Ask her what she thought about one of the sacrament talks.

Third Base: Use one of Cooper's openers.

Home Run: Get a girl's phone number.

A LEAGUE OF THEIR OWN

Weighing six hundred pounds is a romance killer for guys. I know, you think men are so shallow because all they seem to care about is what a girl looks like. Now come on, you have similar feelings about their appearance. You wouldn't be interested if your man never washed his hair, smelled like a urinal, or weighed more than your car either, right?

I know single women who think a man should love her just the way she is. He should, but he has to get to know you first. Before he gets to know you, he has to be attracted to you. Men are visual. They're wired that way. You can get angry about that fact and drown your sorrows in more ice cream or you can do something about it. First impressions count.

Wives, how do you think your husband feels when he comes home after a hard day's work to a woman wearing baggy sweats with her greasy hair pulled back in a ponytail? He wants to want you. Show some effort.

Chapter 6

EYES *on the* BALL

FLIRTING YOUR WAY TO A FIRST DATE

Most girls want you to make the move. They have watched dozens of chick flicks where the handsome man locks eyes with the beautiful woman and he instantly knows it's true love. He falls all over himself to meet her and win her heart. Yeah, we girls eat that stuff up. The only problem is that most guys don't know it's true love, let alone that the girl is trying to give signs that she's interested.

My section in this chapter is going to be super short because Cooper has some practical tips to help you read the signs. It's easier than you think and actually pretty fun. My most important tips are to be observant, playful, and confident. You can do this!

COACH COOPER

INDICATORS OF INTEREST

Guys sometimes find it difficult to tell if a girl is really interested in them. Generally, it's pretty simple. If you ask her out and she says she's busy or comes up with some excuse to not go, she's not interested. For example, "I'm super busy this whole week studying and work is killing me. Sorry." If she's interested, she'll make time to go out with you. But what if she really is busy? If she's busy a certain night but genuinely wants to go out with you, she will suggest another time that works for her.

Recognizing indicators of interest (IOIs) is one of my favorite parts of The Game. I love seeing them, maybe just because I used to be so bad at recognizing them. Men are classically bad at recognizing the signs of when a woman is attracted to them. Because women are generally more socially in tune, they wonder why we can't see what seems obvious to them.

I went through lots of books and videos on body language and found that recognizing IOIs is just like any other skill. It takes practice. Read through this list of IOIs and watch for them in your own interactions with women as well as with your friends or strangers. Once you get good, you'll be able to let your friends know when a girl is attracted to them and they'll definitely appreciate that. More important, you'll feel more confident when talking to women because it will be easy to tell when they're actually attracted to you.

Flicking the hair: When men are in the same area as women, the women's body language will change. They will start casually flicking their hair. It's basically a form of preening (like a bird that cleans its feathers), and women do it when they are trying to be more attractive.

Running hand through hair: Another more obvious version of the same thing, women will subconsciously run their fingers through their hair and brush their hair to the side when they are attracted to someone.

Making eye contact: This is pretty basic. If a girl makes eye contact with you several times—especially if she looks down slightly or smiles after your eyes meet—she's saying she's interested. If your eyes meet and she looks to the side, she's probably just scanning the room and not projecting interest.

Scratching the back of the hand, shoulder, collarbone, or side of face: I don't really know the reasons behind this one, but it definitely works as a sign that she's interested. Look for it. Now, she may truly have an itch, but if the other signs are also present, go for it.

Laughing and tilting head: If she is laughing, she is showing interest, especially if she laughs often or if what you said wasn't all that funny. She may tilt her head as well, which is meant to show that she's playful. In general, if she's showing an unusual amount of interest in what you're saying, she's probably interested.

Pointing the body and feet: You can often gauge interest by whether her body is facing yours or is angled in a different direction. If her shoulders are square toward your body, she's probably pretty engaged in what you're saying. If her body is facing elsewhere, she's looking for a reason to leave and her body is saying that's where she wants to go. If she's a shy girl, however, she might be interested but flirts in a different way. A shy girl might face away from you and just send flirty glances in your direction.

When talking with a group of people, look at a woman's feet. Even if we're not looking directly at someone, our feet will often point toward the person we are interested in. Next time you're interacting with a group that includes a girl you're particularly interested in, look down at your feet. Even if one foot is pointed away from the circle, there's a good chance your other foot is pointed right at the girl you're interested in.

Touching: This is one of the most obvious IOIs. Flirtatious touching is too easy to recognize. Women find excuses to touch you when they're interested—most likely your shoulder or arm at first. While sitting, she may slide right next to you to point at something or show you something on her phone. If she's interested, there will definitely be some physical contact. If she's not, she'll keep a safe distance. Either way, she's trying to gauge your interest based on how you react to her touch and she's being pretty obvious about it (if you recognize it, that is). Again, keep in mind that shyer girls won't be this obvious. There's a good chance you'll have to make the first move.

After I had been dating a particular girl for several months, she asked when it was I first realized she liked me. I explained what IOIs were and pointed out that she kept playing with her hair and touching my arm on our first couple dates. She said she hadn't noticed, but after thinking about it, she said, "Yeah, I think I do that with all the guys I'm interested in."

Mirroring: This one is subtle but easy to recognize if you know what you're looking for. Chances are you've been doing it since you were a kid and just didn't realize it. Mirroring is exactly what it sounds like. It's copying someone else's body position or movements. If you're sitting next to someone you respect or look up to and they're leaning back with a foot on their knee, there's a good chance you're sitting the same way but didn't even notice. This works in The Game of attraction as well. A woman who is attracted to you will mirror your body position. If you're at dinner and you've got your hands sitting on the table a certain way and notice she's holding her hands the same way, that's a good IOI.

You can test a girl's interest with mirroring. If I've gotten an IOI or two and want to be sure she's interested, I'll reach up and scratch my nose or cheek. She will often scratch her face just a moment later, totally unaware that she subconsciously told me she's interested.

Dilating pupils: Scientifically speaking, dilated pupils are a strong indicator of physical attraction. If you notice your date's pupils are dilated, she's into you and probably ready to be kissed. Even if you don't want to go in for a kiss, you at least know that she's attracted to you, which is a confidence booster.

With that in mind, dilated pupils don't always translate to interest. For example, our pupils expand when it's dark in order to capture more light, and our pupils also naturally dilate when we see something we like. Women's pupils will dilate when they look at pictures of babies, or a hungry person's dilate when he sees an appetizing meal. So if your date is looking at you with eyes as big as saucers, check behind you real quick. If there's no cute baby behind you, you're doing something right.

Next time you kiss a girl, if you're not completely caught up in the moment, look at her eyes. Assuming she wanted to be kissed, check to see if her pupils are dilated. I'll bet you a dollar they are. Cool, right? (Now, I'm not actually betting anyone a dollar. I don't want to get a phone call in the middle of the night asking for payment. I'll probably tell you to become a better kisser.)

Leaning forward: Leaning forward indicates interest while leaning backward indicates disinterest. A great technique for generating attraction is leaning forward and backward while talking with a girl you're interested in. After she's says something you find interesting, you lean in and respond with, "No way, you like squirrels too? I love squirrels!" If she leans back a little, you lean back. As the conversation continues, repeat the same thing. Lean in at some interesting point and then lean back again. When she begins to lean in at the same time you do, you've generated some attraction and you can tell she's comfortable getting closer to you.

STATS

- "51% percent of single people surveyed say that flattery is the best way to attract someone."[28]
- 63 percent of married couples claim to have found their mates through a network of friends.[29]

- Some people suggest waiting until the third date to cook someone dinner at home. The first two dates should be on "neutral" ground, not where either of you live.
- The number one relationship argument is over money.

ASSIGNMENTS

First Base: To solidify these concepts, watch some YouTube videos about body language.

Second Base: Compliment three girls today.

Third Base: Make a girl laugh. It's got to be a real laugh, though, not a pity laugh.

Home Run: Play "Go" with some of your guy friends tonight.

A LEAGUE OF THEIR OWN

If you're dealing with a shy guy, give him a break. Let him know you're interested in him. More often than not, he doesn't realize you're interested and just assumes you're being nice.

Most girls spend hours analyzing every word that comes out of a guy's mouth or every move he makes. You're overthinking it. Guys are pretty simple. They're just trying to get up the nerve to say anything to you, so they're not going to be as smooth and romantic as you're used to seeing in chick flicks. Relax and have fun.

Talking to girls is really stressful for guys, especially for young ones who are new to the game of romance. We are alien creatures they're a little bit afraid of. If he's beating around the bush and trying to gather the courage to ask you out, you could say something like, "If you wanted to ask me out, I'd say yes," or, "I would love to try that new frozen yogurt place. Would you like to go with me sometime?" Guys love it when you're direct. You always have the option of asking him out. I was too traditional to ever do that, but it's something worth considering if that's your style. Most guys would be flattered, and it would take the pressure off.

Chapter 7

THE BALL CLUB

WHY GIRLS RUN IN PACKS AND HOW YOU CAN JOIN

Girls run in packs. You've probably already realized that. For example, when you go out to dinner or a dance with a group of other couples, all of the girls suddenly go to the restroom together. Yes, they're capable of going by themselves, but going together serves a purpose. Women's restrooms are where the girls can talk freely about you guys and how the date is going. It's where they can get feedback from their friends.

Your date may like you, but if her friends are hesitant, then she may rethink that good-night kiss. She wants her friends to validate that you're a great guy. Remember, girls can see the big picture, so she has already envisioned all of you hanging out together on special occasions and holidays for the rest of your lives. If her friends don't like you, that ruins the "happily ever after" scenario for her.

Here's the thing: girls *have* to talk. In an average day, women use 143,783 words. Men have already used up their allotted 12,432 words by 3:00 p.m. Okay, that may be a bit exaggerated, but not by much. Talking about everything is how women process information.

Girls need a "girls' day out" with their friends. They *need* girl friends. You don't want to be—nor can you be—everything to her. Besides, do you really want to talk about the finer details between brushed nickel faucets and brass ones? Encourage her to talk to her friends about it for hours on end. Don't use that as an excuse to not listen or she'll think you don't care. Maybe you don't care. Tough. You still have to listen.

All's fair in love; make sure you have "guys' night out" with your bros too. You need time with the guys for different reasons. You're not going to talk and talk and talk. That's probably one reason why you *do* need it.

Elder Bednar recently spoke at a BYU Education Week and challenged attendees to flood the world with our testimonies of Christ on social media. Did you notice that he said testimonies and not relationship updates? Be careful what you share about your relationship online. What happens online stays online. Think twice before you change your relationship status on Facebook. Keep other people out of your relationship.

COACH COOPER

SOCIAL VALUE

The concept I'm about to explain is something that you've probably known about since you were a kid but didn't quite understand the reasons behind it. It's the reason we naturally follow certain people. It's the reason certain kids were popular in middle school. It's the reason one lucky guy you know always has girls chasing him. It has everything to do with dating and it applies to every dating principle that we'll talk about. I'm not talking about your value as a person. We know that the worth of *every* soul is great in the sight of God (see D&C 18:10). I'm talking about your social value, which is the value other people see in you as well as the value you see in yourself.

The man of low social value is constantly trying to do things to get women to like him. The man of high social value doesn't try to convince girls to date him; he simply invites them to join him in fun activities. He may even try to tell women that they shouldn't want to date him, but he quickly learns that telling a girl not to want him only makes them want him more. (I'll tell you more about the disqualification strategy in chapter 9.) He knows himself and what he likes, and he can focus on finding a woman that complements him instead of putting all his effort into convincing a woman to like him.

If you want to break social value down to a primitive level, imagine you are living in a primitive society: no technology, just hunting, gathering, and living in a small tribe. The most valuable

men in this society are the best providers and protectors. The tribal leader holds the highest value because the other men follow him. The woman who wins a place next to the tribal leader can be assured protection because all of the other men in the tribe will protect her as well. Her future is secure because she is with a man of high social value.

Now let's bring it back to the modern world. Social value is just as important. Women are still attracted to a leader of men. Remember that phrase: *leader of men*. That's who you should strive to be. Today, being a tribal leader just means being the leader of a group. If you are the leader of your group of friends, girls will recognize that and will find themselves attracted to it.

One of my favorite experiences at BYU was leading a team of ROTC guys in national and international endurance competitions. They were all great guys, and being a part of that team rewarded me with some of the best times I had at BYU. I noticed, however, that being the leader of a team was attractive to women. I wasn't the best-looking, coolest, or funniest guy on the team, but when I was the team captain, girls seemed much more interested. Leadership is attractive.

There is a little bit of truth behind the stereotype that every girl wants to go out with the high school football team captain. It doesn't matter what he looks like. He's a leader of men! And girls want to be with a tribal leader.

You know how girls make lists of the qualities they want their dream guy to have? You should have done the same thing after reading chapter 2. Every quality that a girl puts on her list is something that holds value to her, and the man that has all of these qualities will have extremely high value in her eyes.

Now that you understand what social value is, you're probably saying to yourself, "Okay, I get it. Right now you're just telling me I should have high social value. But how do I do that?"

I'm glad you asked. All of the chapters following this are really just techniques to increase your social value. As you read about preselection, disqualification, approaching, and playing social games, remember that underneath each aspect, you're really just demonstrating higher value.

DEMONSTRATIONS OF HIGHER AND LOWER VALUE

This section will be talking about demonstration of higher value (DHV) and demonstration of lower value (DLV). You can demonstrate high value through words or through actions. Storytelling can be a great way to demonstrate value with words. We all know what it's like to listen to people brag about their life and tell everyone how awesome they are. It's super unattractive and most people (especially women) are repulsed by individuals who blatantly try to show off and brag. Bragging is a DLV and demonstrates insecurity because it usually means, "I don't think I have enough value to be a part of this group, so I'm going to try to convince them I'm really valuable." When you're storytelling, the DHV has to be subsurface of the story you tell. The second you sound like you're trying to show off, you're hurting yourself.

An example of a DHV could be, "There was this little old lady in my family's ward. She lost the key to her garage, was locked out, and couldn't get to her things. She lived in a senior citizen community and all the garages were separate from the homes. She asked me to pick the lock for her. After I spent some time on it, it finally popped open. I lifted the garage door up, she looked inside, and in a confused little old lady voice, she said, 'Those aren't my things.' I had broken into her neighbor's garage. Apparently, hers was the next one over, totally unlocked."

The point of these stories is to tell about something that's funny or entertaining, and it happens to demonstrate a good quality you have, whether it's caring about helping people or a certain talent you have. We all have good stories to tell. Even your story about some crazy prank you pulled in high school demonstrates a certain type of value. Storytelling is a valuable quality in itself. If you're not a good storyteller, listen to those who are and pay attention to how they use their voices to capture everyone's attention. If a friend tells a good story about you or just compliments you while talking to a girl, he has verbally increased your value and made you more attractive. These are great friends, and the best way to get your friends to talk you up is to talk *them* up in front of other people. Always introduce your friends by mentioning something great about them. Don't just say, "This is my friend Bill." Say, "This is Bill. He has a degree in nuclear engineering, and he's one of the smartest guys I know," or, "This is Josh. He's one of the few people I'd trust with my life."

While story DHVs are good, the best DHV is something you demonstrate in person. Actions are more powerful than words. Confidently walking up to a girl and telling her you thought she looked cute or interesting and you wanted to meet her is a DHV because it shows confidence. Walking into a room with a cute girl on each arm is a DHV. Making people laugh is a DHV. Not being affected by insults, whether playful or real, is a DHV.

Now, what are some examples of DLVs that we do as men? Here is one example: A girl asks what type of music you like and you say, "I like most things, especially techno and hip hop, but I can't stand country music."

She says, "Oh my gosh, I love country music! That's what I grew up on."

"Oh. Yeah, I mean, it's okay. There are a lot of country songs I like. I just don't listen to it that often."

If you're changing your opinions to match a girl's, that's a big DLV. It looks like you have low value and you're willing to be whatever she wants in order to earn her approval. Just hold your ground and you can flirtatiously tease each other about the music you each like. I promise, it'll turn out better that way.

Here's another example: You ask a girl out for a Friday night date. She's busy that night, but suggests Saturday instead. You say, "Oh, I was going to do something that night with a group of friends. Are you free any other night this week?" She's not. "Okay, well let's plan for Saturday night then." Now she's thinking you're willing to ditch your friends to go on a date with her. You've used a DLV on yourself by telling her you're willing to change your plans and bail on your friends in order to spend time with her. You're saying she holds more value to you than your friends do, and you barely even know her. You've also lowered your friends' value, so she won't think much of them if she ever meets them.

TESTS

Women test you partly to determine your social value and confidence, partly to ensure you're compatible with them, and partly because they want you to work to win their affection. Women have always tested men. It's not even conscious most of the time. It's just hardwired into them. They want to know what you're made of and if you're really the confident macho man you seem to be.

Years ago, I had a friend who had eleven older sisters, so because of this unique perspective, I asked him what the secret to understanding the female mind was. He said, "You know what women really want? They want you to tell them what they want." It was funny at the time, but there's some truth behind what he said. Women want a man who knows what he wants, and a lot of their tests are designed to determine whether you know what *you* want. Do you find yourself saying, "Let's do what you want," trying to get in a girl's good graces? Or are you a man who finds himself saying, "I want to see a movie. Care to join me?" The latter is more attractive.

If we dive into these tests more, dating experts have divided them into two kinds: compliance tests and congruence tests. Women will put you through compliance tests to determine your value.[32] A girl you just met may ask you to get her something, a bottle of water, for example. It might even be right next to her, and so it seems like a ridiculous request. There's nothing wrong with doing something nice, but if you get the water for her, you're putting yourself in a position where you are complying with her requests and working for her approval. The better course of action is to say something playful like, "Okay, but it's going cost you. I'll trade you a bottle of water for an embarrassing story about yourself." Turn the tables so she is working to pass your tests and win

your affection instead. If she's asking for compliance, trade for compliance. If she says, "Wait right here while I go into this store," try responding with, "I'm actually going to check out that store over there," or, "Okay, but only if you give me a kiss on the cheek."

Congruence tests, on the other hand, are meant to test your confidence and shake you up a bit.[33] Some of them might have you at a loss for words. Some that girls might use are, "So, you came all the way over here to hit on me?" or, "What's with the goofy shirt?"

First off, if she's giving you a test, she is already attracted to you and would love for you to pass her tests so she can finally find her dream guy. The way to handle congruence tests is to ignore the playful insult and turn it around: "I just met you. Why don't you tell me why I should hit on you?" or, "You like the shirt, huh? You must have been checking me out." Of course, the way you say it should be playful. Women love when you can dish it right back. Playful marriages are healthy marriages.

The key is to just be confident and not let anything she says affect you. This same principle is being repeated a lot because it's important. Be confident and know what you want.

STATS

- "On average, daters will kiss on the second date."[34]
- "A woman can increase the likelihood of a man approaching her if she uncrosses her arms, makes subtle eye contact, and smiles."[35]
- "Italian food is one of the most popular restaurants for a first date."[36]

ASSIGNMENTS

First Base: Invite another couple to go out with you so she has another female to chat with during the evening.

Second Base: Encourage her to have a "girls' night."

Third Base: Ask her if you can meet her friends. Do *not* talk about how cute they are. You are, however, allowed to talk about their positive personality traits you admire. Careful, though; don't make her feel like you're interested in them or that she has to compete with them.

Home Run: If you're in a relationship, plan a "girls' night" for her and her friends. If you're married, take the kids out so she can stay in with her friends or you can be the babysitter so she can go out. You can *really* knock it out of the ballpark if you plan the night, decorate the home, clean up, cook the food or make the snacks, and get each of the women some flowers. Sounds overboard, right? Hey, it's a home run. What did you expect?

A LEAGUE OF THEIR OWN

Girls, make it easier for guys to approach you. Don't always huddle in packs. Anything a girl does to shake a guy's confidence is amplified when there are ten girls watching him try to make his move. It's bad enough if he geeks out and you laugh, but if you're standing there with a bunch of your friends who are also laughing at him, he'll never try again. If you're at a dance or social event, wander off to the drinking fountain by yourself so that he can try to talk to you alone. Make eye contact with him to encourage him to try.

Chapter 8

THE UNIFORM

HOW TO LOOK LIKE A KNIGHT IN SHINING ARMOR

You only get one. "One what?" you ask. You only get one chance to make a first impression? One chance to find your soul mate? One chance to win the lottery? No, something much more significant: you only get one body. One of the most important characteristics that women look at is how you take care of yourself.

In this society of quick fixes and throw-away purchases, it's easy to replace almost anything. Even with the amazing medical technologies and advances of plastic surgery that allow us to replace certain body parts (have you seen most of the celebrities lately?), you still only get one body. It comes with a lifetime warranty, but the quality is not guaranteed. That is up to you. How you treat it carries the marks of abuse, misuse, or respect.

You've heard the phrase "cleanliness is next to godliness," right? Here's a little self-evaluation health quiz to see if there are some areas where you can take better care of your precious temple. Circle YES or NO.

- I bathe at least every other day and change into clean clothes daily.

  YES NO
- I brush my teeth twice a day.

  YES NO
- I have up-to-date vaccinations.

  YES NO
- I wash my hands often and always before eating.

  YES NO
- I retire to bed early.

  YES NO
- I arise early.

  YES NO
- I sleep six to eight hours each night.

  YES NO
- I engage in strenuous physical activity at least three times a week.

  YES NO
- I try to arrange my time so I walk more than I ride or sit.

  YES NO
- I am careful about how much candy and soda I consume.

  YES NO
- I drink six to eight glasses of water each day.

  YES NO
- I abstain from alcohol, tobacco, tea, coffee, and harmful drugs.

  YES NO
- I feel fit and strong.

  YES NO

- I obey the Word of Wisdom.

  YES NO

- I eat five servings of fruits and vegetables a day.

  YES NO

When I was a little girl, I had a Primary teacher explain to me that I only had to decide once in my life whether or not I would smoke or drink alcohol. I only had to choose one time whether I wanted the words *smoker* or *drinker* to describe me. That made sense to me. Once I decided not to partake of such harmful substances, I wouldn't have to think about it ever again. My teacher handed each one of us a card upon which we could write our commitments to ourselves about living the Word of Wisdom. I still have that card and have been true to my promise ever since.

Keeping the Word of Wisdom is really a no-brainer. We know that taking drugs and drinking alcohol is bad for our bodies. So don't use them. You know this. The temptation occurs when someone cool asks you to do it. You are way cooler if you don't. Trust me. Of course, the Word of Wisdom is about not just what *not* to partake of but how to better care for your body and soul. It's a great rule book for how to suit up for The Game.

Cooper is going to tell you some great details about male style. Find out what clothing styles work best for your physical assets and personality.

In a society that values beauty more than health, it is no surprise that increasing depression rates and plummeting self-image are the results. I have met hundreds of single adults who question and doubt the inherent beauty of their body and personal value. Too much emphasis is placed on what the mirror tells us about physical beauty and how our value in society is determined by that judgment. Do you judge your personal worth by your reflection from a piece of glass? You realize it doesn't tell the whole story of you, right?

God created many wonderful things: plants, animals, fish, fowl, flowers, trees. *Then* He created you. He didn't just say you were His finest creation; He said you were *family*. Be gentle with yourself.

COACH COOPER

STYLE AND FASHION

Fashion is always changing, but looking good and having a sense of style is something that doesn't change much. If you look at old pictures of your grandpa, he probably had style and dressed nice, even if the fashions of the day were way different. I'm not going to give you fashion advice because that could change next year, but I will give you some advice on looking good. You may not care how you look, but women do. They care a lot more than we do, and they notice the little details in how a person is dressed.

You can't judge a book by its cover, but if the cover doesn't look good, then you'll probably never look at what's inside. Appearances and first impressions aren't everything, but project a good first impression and a lot more women will want to see what's inside.

Whether you have never given a second thought to your appearance or you consider yourself a fashion guru, here are a few ways to improve your appearance:

Buy clothes that fit. If you wear clothes that are too small or too baggy, you're doing yourself a disservice. The most common fitting problem we have as men is to buy clothes that are too big. Why? Because loose-fitting clothes are comfortable. Well, guess what? They're making you look sloppy and fat. It can often be difficult to find clothes that have a personal fit when you're buying clothes right off the rack. That white collared shirt you wore on your mission could probably fit two of you inside it. Am I right? Take a shirt or suit you like to a tailor and pay the money to have it fitted. You will look like a new man. Clothing stores often sell shirts that come in different fits, like modern, slim, or extra slim. Try these on and ask a girl in the store or a friend which looks

best on you. If you simply wear clothes that fit, you will completely change the way you look. You will have a more manly appearance, and you'll feel more confident because you know you look good.

Hit the gym and start eating right. If you're overweight or too skinny, you're not projecting an image of strength or manliness. Think carefully about the kind of food you put in your body to fuel it. Regardless of what you do, your physical body is an important part of who you are, and so you need to have the discipline to take care of it every day and give it the exercise it needs, just like you should do with your spirit every day. Plus, you'll feel more confident each day you become more fit. When it comes to how you eat, a plant-based diet will make you healthier than you knew was possible. It is now scientifically proven that the Word of Wisdom is true.

Have proper hygiene. I have to mention this because the truth is, some guys just don't know or care how to take care of their man stink. Shower every day. Shave. Use deodorant. Trim the nose hair. In a study, 93 percent of women said they didn't like much back hair.[39] The point is, you want to look clean and groomed. Something else you may want to look into is cologne. Do some research before buying cologne, and go for quality. Make sure you don't overdo it. Spray a little mist in the air and walk into it before you put a shirt on. If you spray yourself point-blank, the smell might be overpowering. You don't want people to notice it from far away. Think of it this way: if you can only smell it when you're up close, you're encouraging that special lady to stay nearby once she notices it.

IMPROVE YOUR STYLE

Be bold and try something you normally wouldn't do. Go to the mall and find a store with men's clothing you like. Find a stylish female employee and tell her you're looking to change your style and try something new. Say that you noticed she had a good sense of fashion so you thought you would ask for her help. She'll be thrilled. Go at a time in the day when they're not busy so all her attention can be focused on you. Ask her to help you pick out an outfit and be open to her recommendations, but don't compromise your own opinion. This exercise will help you overcome shyness, if that's an issue, but it will also teach you to be open to new things, and you'll end up with an outfit you look good in. If she picks out things you can't afford, make a mental note of the clothing she picked and find something similar but cheaper elsewhere.

My last bit of advice is to get online and look up sites that cover men's fashion and grooming. There is some really great stuff out there.

Some people have called meeting girls "Real Life Gaming" because every interaction with a girl is like starting a video game at level one and then advancing through different stages. If you lose the girl at level five, you have to start over at the beginning with the next girl you approach. This game is way more fun than any video game I've ever heard of though.

As you improve yourself, especially if it is drastic or fast, some friends may get upset and try to discourage you. Psychologically speaking, you fill a certain spot in their reality, and it might be uncomfortable for them to change that. Also, no one likes to feel like they're being left behind, because then they are forced to ask themselves why they aren't making improvements like you are.

If you have female friends and you're in the "friend zone," then it's even more likely that they won't like what's happening. She may see it as one of her male friends no longer competing for her interest. Just work on making the best you.

PEACOCKING

If girls notice every detail (and they do), then here's a way you single guys can use that to your advantage.

This is an old, popular technique. When a man goes out, he wears something completely ridiculous (like a giant fuzzy hat, goggles, or platform shoes) so that women have an excuse to come up and talk to him.

I gave it a try, but I went for something much more conservative. Recognizing you should dress to attract the kind of women you're looking for, I decided I would wear a nice wood watch, as opposed to a huge fur hat. It achieved the desired effect, and women came up to me to comment on it. As a guy, you probably don't pay much attention to little things like that. But women are all about jewelry and the small details in what they wear, so naturally they quickly noticed an interesting watch.

If you're wearing something unique, you'll get bonus points if there's a story behind it. I could explain that the watch, for example, reminded me of home because of the type of wood it was made of. Teak wood holds up well near the ocean and doesn't get damaged by the salt water like other woods do. Now we can talk about woodworking and growing up near the ocean, or I can ask her about her childhood.

STATS

- "A woman has wider ranging peripheral vision, which allows her to check out a man's body from head to toe without getting caught. A male's peripheral vision is poorer, which is why a man will move his gaze up and down a woman's body in an obvious way. Men do not ogle more than women—their tunnel vision just causes them to get caught more easily."[40]
- "A woman is instinctively four times more likely to mirror another woman than a man is to mirror another man. Additionally, while women also mirror men's body language, men are reluctant to mirror a woman's gestures or posture unless he is in courtship mode."[41]

- "The 'face platter,' or when people place one hand on top of the other and rest [the] faces on top of the hands, is often used in courtship. It's used mainly by women . . . who want to attract a man's attention. Their face is placed as if it were on a platter for the other person to admire."[42]
- "Studies show that women laugh at men they're attracted to, and men are attracted to women who laugh at them. From a man's perspective, saying a woman has a good sense of humor doesn't mean she makes jokes; it means she laughs at his jokes."[43]
- "In a survey conducted by Match.com, 43% said fresh breath mattered the most before a date, 17% said stylish clothes, 15% said sexy fragrance, 14% said good skin, and 10% said great hair."[44]

ASSIGNMENTS

First Base: Ask a girl you trust to tell you how you look.

Second Base: Buy a new tailored shirt.

Third Base: Take a few extra minutes to style your hair. See how girls respond.

Home Run: Resolve to eat healthier and start a consistent exercise routine.

A LEAGUE OF THEIR OWN

My dear young sisters, because you are to be a cocreator with God, He needs to use you as His instrument in a very *physical* way: have babies, serve others, clean someone's house when they're sick, take meals to people, and so on. Take care of your bodies so that they will be strong for these mortal tasks.

Be gentle with your bodies and learn to listen to them. They will tell you when something is wrong. What you put into your body is reflected on the outside of your body. Eat healthy, exercise, sweat, inhale deeply, and drink lots of water.

Exercise can help beat depression. It can be especially important for girls who suffer with PMS. Women are 70 percent more likely than men to suffer from depression.[45] Depression can be caused by a chemical imbalance in your body, fluctuating hormones, or Satan trying to make you less effective so you aren't a force for good in the world.

If you're feeling low, remember that the sun has a sinking spell every night, but it keeps coming back up every morning!

Chapter 9

FOUL BALL

WHAT A GIRL THINKS WHEN YOU FART

Why is this chapter in the book? Because *every* woman I talked to begged me to mention it. That's how strongly they feel about this.

You're up at bat. You hit the ball. The wind catches it and prevents it from flying very far. You're not able to get to first base before being tagged out. Farting is the dating equivalent.

Farting: Women are simply not amused by passing gas like guys are. If she laughs, it's only because she can't believe what a child you are. Women want to be treated like a lady in your presence, not like one of your buddies. Is that too much to ask? When you fart or belch, you're telling her, "You're not important to me. You're not a lady. I don't respect you enough to behave myself in front of you." Who knew so much was said in a single fart? Remember, she wants to be proud of you in front of her friends and family, not embarrassed. Every time you act like an uncivilized animal in front of her, she's reconsidering her choice to be with you. Save it for the locker room.

"Yeah, but those are natural body functions," you weakly state to defend yourself. If you *must*, then simply excuse yourself and do it somewhere else. That's what bathrooms are for. And don't come back trailing odors. Think I'm being too harsh here? Somebody's got to tell you the truth.

This goes for you married guys too. One of the great things about being married is that you have someone who will love you forever, despite your flaws. While that's true, it doesn't mean you can be a complete slob. You might think that gives you the right to let loose, or let one loose. Marriage is not a free pass to pass gas. Yes, she loves you, but you lose more than points every time you fart in front of her. You showed control while you were dating (at least I hope), so have some self-respect and consideration for her by controlling your bodily functions.

Belching: Unless you live in a foreign country where belching after a meal is considered polite, it's not. Learn good table manners at home so that when you're out on a date, your proper etiquette will kick in automatically and you'll be able to concentrate more on the girl and treating her like a lady. Practice on your mom or your sister. Practice good dinner conversation. Have a few jokes tucked away in your head.

Batting errors: Here are other batting errors that will prevent you from scoring with a woman:

- Forgetting her name
- Picking your nose
- Cutting her off when she's trying to talk
- Adjusting your crotch in public
- Not taking care of your body odor
- Leaving stains on your clothes
- Keeping the toilet seat up
- Leaving your dishes on the table and expecting her to take care of them

- Looking at, texting, answering your phone while she's talking
- Answering your phone while you're eating dinner at a restaurant
- Treating others with disdain (even if you treat your girl well, she'll notice how you treat others too)
- Talking bad about other people

A girl wants you to be yourself around her, but you should be your *best* self. She wants you to be her knight in shining armor, not the squire who steps in horse poop all day. Learn to be a gentleman.

When I was in high school, I went to Mexico as an exchange student. I had been to Tijuana for a day with my dad when I was younger and discovered the fun of bargaining with the locals for souvenirs, but I had never lived in a foreign country before. My exchange trip was just for the summer months because I didn't want to leave my family for an entire school year.

I stayed with a wonderful family in Culiacan, Sinaloa, in Mexico. One night, my exchange sister and her boyfriend set me up with their friend to go on a double date. The boy was a true gentleman and tried to walk on the outside of the sidewalk to protect me from cars on the street. (Guys, did you know that was a thing? Yep, you're supposed to do that to be chivalrous. Girls will be impressed.) Unfortunately, I didn't know that at the time.

It was a hot summer night, which meant cockroaches were everywhere. As I hopped around the sidewalk trying to dodge the disgusting insects in my path, I didn't realize that my poor date was edging closer and closer onto the street and in the way of oncoming traffic. He was trying so hard to be a gentleman! Poor guy. I was so oblivious.

Here are a few more ways how to be a real gentleman:

- *Always* open her door (not just on the first date, and not just until the wedding).
- When a woman enters a room, stand up.

- Always introduce her when you are talking to friends or family she doesn't know.
- When walking upstairs with a woman, follow behind her in case she falls back.
- When walking downstairs with a woman, go in front of her in case she falls forward.
- When walking with a woman on a sidewalk, walk on the outer edge closest to the street to protect her from oncoming cars.

Once you fart in front of a woman, you're disqualified. You just lost points. Can I make this any clearer? Cooper is going to talk about two fascinating concepts: disqualification and preselection. Pay attention.

COACH COOPER

Okay, I think my mom hit it pretty hard about not farting. Let's assume you have solved that problem and moved on to more interesting concepts. The next thing I'll talk about is one of the *keys* to attracting women. Once you have it, women will come to you instead of you chasing them.

PRESELECTION

This principle states that women are attracted to men whom other women are attracted to. It's such a simple and powerful principle. Imagine that you're at some fun social gathering. You look around and see the world's best looking man standing in the corner of the room by himself. You look around more and see an average-looking guy in the center of the room surrounded by women who are laughing and hanging on his every word. Several are flirtatiously touching his shoulder and clearly vying for his attention. You've probably forgotten about the world's best looking man by now, and so has every other girl in the room. Any girl who walks in will naturally be more attracted to average Joe because everybody else seems to be.

Women come into contact with dozens or possibly even hundreds of men every day of their lives. There's no way they can get to know the personality and ambitions of every one of those men, so the most efficient way for the mind to quickly determine which men have the most potential is to choose men that other women are attracted to.

You do the same thing. If you want to watch a good movie, do you independently preview every movie that's ever been made until you find one that has potential? No. If other people are enjoying a movie and it's getting great reviews, you assume you'll enjoy it as well. This doesn't work 100 percent of the time, but it's a good way to narrow down your selection.

So how do you become preselected by women? It's a process. Just talk to women without worrying about dating them. Nothing is more attractive than that. Focus on building a group of friends who are women. Also, the more attractive they are, the more powerful the element of preselection will be. Regardless, when you go out to a friend's party or a Church social event, just have fun with the women there. Don't ignore all the women you're not attracted to. Talk to them and have fun with them too. If anything, it's a good way to practice having fun conversations without feeling nervous.

Use some of the conversation ideas we cover in this book. When a girl sees that her friends are laughing and having a good time talking to a you, she will come over and join in the conversation. You may end up with a big group, and you may not. Who cares? What's important is you've made a friend or two, and the next time you see these people, you can instantly connect with them. Better yet, when you show up at a party or event, have some girls with you when you walk through the door. The girls in the room will notice and assume that you are an attractive man (which you are, of course), and the men in the room will be disarmed because they see you as a friend instead of a threat.

The point is, don't worry about trying to attract that one woman you have your eye on yet. Just go out, make friends, and practice being fun and interesting. If women have a positive emotional experience when they're with you, they'll want to be around you again, and so will their friends. The best pickup line is something good said about you from one woman to another.

Here's an easy technique you might be able to use to establish preselection and make your mama proud at the same time. Do you have any female relatives who are similar to you in age and are cute? Bring your sisters or female cousins to a party or any social gathering. You'll walk in the door looking like a champ because you're surrounded by cute girls, and you can go around introducing them to other guys in the room, which is a win-win for everyone. Your female family members are happy they're meeting new guys, the guys in the room love you because you're introducing them to cute girls, and all of the other women in the room now want to meet you.

DISQUALIFICATION

This is one of several counterintuitive principles of creating attraction. Disqualification is basically teasing a girl about why she potentially can't date you. Of course, it has to be more subtle than that, but what you're doing is putting the idea in a girl's head that you don't consider her a potential partner for some reason. You've disqualified her from being on your attraction radar, and she'll have to work to qualify herself as someone you should want to be with.

This is as simple as casually mentioning mid-conversation, "I really like you; it's a shame you're too young for me," or, "You know our problem? We're too similar. We could never get along because we'd drive each other crazy." Don't wait for a response; just continue with the conversation after making the comment. She's going to remember you said it and wonder why.

When I first heard about this, I of course wanted to try it. I explained the idea to a roommate, and we were outside playing volleyball later that day when I saw my opportunity. Next to the volleyball court was a pool. Two cute girls were conveniently swimming and secretly wishing that two young, handsome gentlemen would approach them. It's hard to play volleyball when it's just you and one friend, so we walked over and asked if they wanted to play a game with us.

"No, that's okay. We're not that good anyway." Not interested.

Because disqualification was fresh on my mind, I decided to give it a try. "Oh, okay. If you aren't any good, then we should probably find someone else."

"Well, we're not terrible."

"I don't know. I mean, if you can't play, then you should probably just stay in the water."

"Okay, just give us a minute to dry off and we'll come play."

I was shocked. Could it really be that easy? I would definitely have to do some more field research. Isn't research great?

Here's an example of a technique I learned from a guy who had studied disqualification. I just started a new semester of school and went to the first day of institute. After listening to a gospel lesson, we all went outside to find tables of food and some two hundred young single adults talking to each other, doing their best to play The Game (whether consciously or not).

This particular technique doesn't require knowing anyone. All it requires is the guts to walk up to a group of girls and start a conversation. I didn't know many people because it was the beginning of a new semester, so I found two attractive girls talking together and opened with, "Hey, you two look like you're just standing around waiting for guys to come up and flirt with you."

"Yeah, maybe," they said, laughing.

"You don't have to be old-fashioned and wait around for them to come to you. Come on, let's go find you some guys to talk to."

There were probably a lot of things running through those female minds:

- This guy is obviously confident because approaching a group of girls doesn't faze him.
- He must know a lot of people here if he's going to introduce us to guys.
- Why does he want to introduce us to other guys? Why isn't he trying to hit on us? He must have a lot of options.

At this point, preselection kicked in and four other girls walked up and joined their friends. Their female radar went off when they noticed their friends talking to a guy and giggling, so they were naturally drawn in. I spotted a couple of guys I knew and signaled them to come over and join us, and then I introduced them to the group of girls, telling the girls how great they were.

Talking your buddies up is a win-win because it makes them sound awesome, it demonstrates that you are friends with awesome people, and it's much more attractive to talk other people up than to try to talk yourself up. I ended up with six new girls I could call for a date. Strangely, they weren't as interested in my friends, even after I had talked them up. Remember how leadership is attractive?

In just a few sentences, you can demonstrate that you are confident, a leader of men, preselected by women, and a guy girls want to be with.

STATS

- 88 percent of women find money to be important in a relationship.[47]
- 60 percent of women and 64 percent of men don't talk about politics on a first date.[48]
- 76 percent of women date men that are at least five years older than they are.[49]
- 80 percent of men date women that are at least five years younger than they are.[50]

ASSIGNMENTS

First Base: Stop farting and burping in public.

Second Base: Open doors for women.

Third Base: Open the passenger door on your car for your date.

Home Run: Open the passenger door on your car door for your date and reach over and hand her the seatbelt. This applies to you married guys too.

A LEAGUE OF THEIR OWN

Now girls, you're not perfect roses either. In fact, the way you drown yourself in that rose perfume may be a complete turn-off to the guys. In many instances, it may remind them of their grandmother. Just a little will do fine. Most guys don't like a girl with tons of makeup either. They want to see your natural beauty, not your war paint. Tone it down a notch. While they most definitely want you to be beautiful, they also want a girl they can jump in the pool with and not have to worry that her mascara is going to ink up the water. They don't want a girl who is going to sit on the sidelines because she might break a fingernail. They want to have fun with you.

Chapter 10

WHAT'S *the* CALL?

WHEN YOU CALL HER AND WHEN YOU DON'T

Just pick up the phone and call. It almost doesn't matter what you say. Most girls love to talk, so it shouldn't be that hard. If you tell a girl you're going to call her, do it. If she never hears from you, she will come to one of two conclusions:

- You are a slimeball.
- She is a loser.

Don't do that to her. No one deserves to be treated like that. If you get a girl's number with no intention of calling her, you can simply say something like, "Thanks. If I'm brave enough one day, I just might call you." That way when you don't call her, she'll just think you're a wimp. At least that's better than a slimeball.

You can always start with a playful text and then work your way up to the actual phone call.

When you text, ask yourself, "What would my parents think if they saw what I just wrote?"

One of my sons was dating a sweet nonmember girl in high school. She was always polite and well-mannered around me, and they had a nice friendship. My son even took her to several Church events and started teaching her about the gospel. I always do random checks of texts on my kids' cell phones, and I was satisfied their conversations were innocent and appropriate.

One day, I noticed that her language changed dramatically. He said he didn't know what was going on but that her behavior was also changing. She had gotten involved with a different crowd at school and was headed in a bad direction. The language in the text was the first red flag, and soon after, my son broke up with her. It was sad to see such a sweet girl change so quickly. It was all noticeable in the texts.

Never break up with a girl over a text. Sure, it's a lot easier than facing her in person and trying to explain to her that it's over while tears flow down her cheeks. Don't be a coward. She deserves the common courtesy to hear it from you in person. Be. A. Man. Remember that chapter?

Never send or encourage sexually suggestive texts. *Never* take pictures you wouldn't want your mother to see.

When you're at a family event or with others, show some constraint. Acknowledge that the people in the room with you mean something to you. Connect with them. Talk to them. Be with them. You can always politely excuse yourself to use the restroom for five minutes and get your phone fix there. Join the world. Put your cell phone down, get out there, and live.

Randall L. Ridd, the second counselor of the general Young Men presidency, gave a fantastic talk at the April 2014 general conference about technology. He said, "Owning a smart phone does not make you smart. But using it wisely can."[52]

One final thought on the subject. Have you ever gone out to dinner and noticed a girl sitting at a table, quietly eating her meal, while her date or husband takes a business call on his cell phone? Don't be that guy. He's an insensitive jerk. Life will still go on if you don't answer that phone. Focus on her. If you don't, she'll find someone who will.

Unless you're taking pictures together or texting each other during dinner, keep your cell phones in your pockets.

COACH COOPER

MAKING GOOD CONVERSATION

Have you ever got up the nerve to talk to a cute girl, but after a minute or so, you're not sure what to say? The conversation dies, and one of you comes up with a reason to leave. That's the worst.

I noticed that people tend to have the same conversations with each other. Especially if you're going to college, everyone asks the same three questions when they meet someone: "What's your name?" "Where are you from?" and "What are you studying?" They have good intentions, but it's not creative. I used to do the same thing because I couldn't think of anything better to say to start off a conversation.

There's an easy way to use the same questions but make the conversation one hundred times more interesting: Don't ask. Assume.

That's right. When striking up a conversation with people, instead of asking them where they're from, make an assumption. Saying, "I'll bet you're from California," will make her wonder why you think that, especially if you're right. If you say, "You look like someone who would be a dance major," she'll be intrigued, and you have a much better conversation on your hands.

Don't just take a wild guess. Learn to analyze what she's wearing, the way she carries herself, and the way she talks. The more you practice analyzing and making assumptions, the better you'll get at it. The better you get, the more fun it is. When you assume something and it turns out to be right, you form a connection because she feels like you can see things about her that others can't.

TEXTING VERSUS CALLING

The best way to ask a girl out is to do it is in person. I know it's easier said than done, but try not to be nervous about it. It's not a big deal. It's just a date. She's probably just as nervous as you are.

There's a temptation to use technology to distance ourselves and not feel as nervous. Another good way to ask someone out is over the phone. There's nothing wrong with that. Just don't ask a girl on a first date through a text message. Texting can be fun, but it can't replace actually talking with someone. It's best used as a tool for between dates or to set up an informal time to meet up.

A word about fighting and lack of good communication: If you find yourself in the doghouse or arguing with your girlfriend, then what are you doing? I have a friend who always seemed to be arguing with his girlfriend. I've never been in that situation, so I just don't get it. Eventually, they broke up, and everyone was relieved.

If your relationship is bad while you're dating, it probably won't get any better after you're married. Why not find someone you get along with?

If you're already in a committed relationship, the fighting needs to stop. Be sure you're doing everything you possibly can to keep communications healthy (see chapter 26). If you've done something wrong or if you've been dumb in some way, be a man, admit it, and apologize. If she's just being crazy for no apparent reason, realize that some girls are just immature like that. Look for a woman to date, not just a girl.

STATS

- A study in the journal *Social Influence* found that ladies were more likely to give out their phone numbers to guys who flirted with them on sunny days as opposed to cloudy days. Researchers say people may be in a better mood on sunny days or men may be better flirters in good weather.[53]
- Men were the first to wear high heels around the 1600s. Women began wearing them to look more masculine.[54]
- Women have more taste buds than men.[55]
- Women cry on average between thirty and sixty-four times a year, while men on average cry less than seven times.[56]

ASSIGNMENTS

First Base: Text her.
Second Base: Call her just to say hi and tell her a funny joke.
Third Base: Call to ask her what she thinks about something.
Home Run: Call to invite her to a fun activity.

A LEAGUE OF THEIR OWN

A guy may actually be trying to flirt with you by catching your eye. If you never look up from your cell phone, you might miss the love of your life.

Sending or encouraging sexually suggestive texts is *not* flirtatious fun. It is a red flag that the guy is a sleezeball and not a gentleman. It doesn't say nice things about you either.

Chapter 11

SPORTS MEDICINE

WIN OVER HER HEART AND FUNNY BONE

Laughter can be the best medicine, and its positive effects on your mind and body are no joke. Scores of hospitals and cancer centers around the United States are taking humor seriously enough to create special rooms, television channels, and libraries dedicated to humor.

Comedian-pianist Victor Borge said, "The shortest distance between two people is a smile."[60] Laughter is even better than a smile. Twenty seconds of hearty laughter is equal to five minutes of aerobic rowing. Laughter creates "inner jogging." It's a whole lot easier than running around the track at the gym.

Laughter lifts the spirit and provides an excellent way to connect with other people. Surround yourself with people who are upbeat, fun, and allow you to laugh and be yourself. Marry someone who makes you laugh every day. Life gets stressful once you are married and have bills to pay, mouths to feed, and diapers

to change. You need to be able to laugh until it hurts with your spouse. Life is too hard to take it so seriously.

I love the line in the movie *Who Framed Roger Rabbit?* when Jessica, the gorgeously drawn cartoon character, answers the question on everyone's mind: "Why would a beautiful woman who could have any man in the world want to marry such a goofy rabbit?" She answers in her sexy, deep voice, "He makes me laugh."[61] I'm certainly no bombshell like Jessica, but I agree. My husband is hilarious and makes me laugh every day.

Gorgeous women marry average guys for these reasons:

- He's rich
- He's confident and makes her laugh

Life can get too serious. Be her respite. Men are often much better at being playful than women are. That's one of the things we love about you guys, and that's why we need you in our lives. Boys and men are always ready to play, whereas girls and women think they need to be cleaning something. That's obviously a generality, but there is truth in it.

Laugh a lot, but always be mindful of what or who is the brunt of your jokes. Johann Wolfgang von Goethe said, "Nothing shows a man's character more than what he laughs at."[62] Don't be cruel. What you might think is a funny little joke could hurt a girl's self-esteem for years. Did you hear me? *Never* tease unkindly.

It's also important to be sensitive to her seemingly erratic moods. My dad was always super sensitive around his three daughters, often bringing us flowers and showing unusual patience. I once asked him how it was that he understood how to act around us when we were hormonal or irrational. He said that when he was in high school, he had a girlfriend who was a bubbly cheerleader. Once a month, she would become unusually quiet and sad. He didn't quite understand what was happening to her, but he knew it was something significant. Girls deserve your utmost kindness, even when they seem to be going nuts. They probably are, but it's only temporary.

COACH COOPER

Women are attracted to humor, plain and simple. If you live an impressive life and accomplish a lot, you'll find that women will be much more impressed if you can joke about it and not take yourself too seriously.

Generally, women will ask the same standard questions: "What do you do for a living?" or if you're a student, "What are you studying?" What if you said something like, "I'm a disposable lighter repairman," or, "I paint the stripes on lighthouses." Those should get a laugh (at least as soon as they realize you're not being serious), and it has the added benefit of making them curious about what you really do. Funny and mysterious is a good combination for first meeting someone. Plus, you'll learn if she has a sense of humor.

STATS

- In the 1550s, the verb *flirt* initially meant "to turn up one's nose, sneer at" and then "to rap or flick, as with fingers." In the 1560s, the noun *flirt* had come to mean a woman of "loose behavior."[63]
- There are over fifty-two specific "flirting signals." For women, the most common is the hair flip.[64]
- Studies show that women initiate flirting 90 percent of the time.[65]

- Researchers suggest women wear red-hued lipstick while flirting. A Manchester University study tracked the eye movements of men and found that they looked at red lips for 7.3 seconds and pink for 6.7 seconds.[66]

ASSIGNMENTS

First Base: Memorize a few clean jokes.

Second Base: Find out what tickles her funny bone and make her laugh.

Third Base: Take her to a clean comedy club.

Home Run: Find a running gag that will keep you and your girl laughing for years. Create an inside joke that binds you together. Make her laugh every day.

A LEAGUE OF THEIR OWN

Make *him* laugh. Don't be so serious all the time. So what if the dishes aren't clean or the carpet needs to be vacuumed? Go play with him instead. The planet will still continue to revolve if your house isn't spotless. Be spontaneous and fun. He doesn't want to live with his mother or his business partner. He wants a lover and a best friend. Lighten up.

We all have shortcomings and need to be able to laugh at ourselves. Poking fun at yourself lets others know you don't take yourself too seriously, but be careful not to belittle yourself either.

Keep a joy journal and fill it with jokes, happy memories, and things that will make you smile when you are feeling down. By the way, it's normal to not be happy all the time. Our fluctuating hormones can have a powerful influence on our mood. Be gentle with yourself.

Chapter 12

WORKING *the* INFIELD

COMPLIMENTS AND CHATTER

In baseball, the players on the field must be constantly communicating, whether with words, hand signals, or body language. Players that work well together encourage one another and offer expressions that keep each other motivated. Working the infield in a relationship involves the same type of constant uplifting banter. I'm talking about compliments. Women have an innate longing to be of worth to their man. You will score many points when your woman hears you say, "I couldn't have done it without you!" or "I owe it all to you!" She wants to be the wind beneath your wings.

Remember the old adage, "Behind every successful man is a supportive woman." She wants you to be successful, and she wants to feel like she helped you get there. All people, not just women, want to feel like they make a difference in this world. Let her know when she's helped you, and she'll be more than willing to do it again. She wants to feel like you two are an unstoppable team that can do great things together.

Proverbs 23:7 says, "For as he thinketh in his heart, so is he." In this case, "she." If you give her a lovely idea of herself, that's how she will become. The time will come when she will accept your estimate of her as her estimate of herself. Men don't realize that most women have low self-esteem and a lifetime of insecurities. Let her know *why* you love her. She may not even recognize her characteristics or talents as being special or different.

My husband used to always compliment me on my beautiful skin. I thought that was such a strange compliment because it was, after all, just skin. When I looked closer and compared my husband's freckled skin to my clear olive complexion, I understood better why he valued it so much. He grew up with skin he considered to be less than ideal, and I had never given mine a second thought. If you like something about your woman, let her know. Be specific. She will undoubtedly return the compliment. Your kind words may help her to see herself in a new way, improving her overall self-esteem.

I think it's safe to say that most women are not completely happy with their bodies. Every woman can find something about her body that she would readily change if she could. A woman will feel sexier when she knows she is beautiful in your eyes. Tell her specifically what it is that you love about her: her beautiful eyes, great smile, perfect teeth, adorable toes, or whatever. She wants to feel feminine and beautiful, like a desirable woman. You are guaranteed a positive response when you let her know you think she is one of nature's finest creations.

A word of caution, however: don't compliment her *only* on her physical appearance. Be sure to let her know that you think what's inside is even more beautiful. Every woman worries that when her beauty fades, the man she's with will dump her for a younger, prettier version.

Women will analyze every word you say, as well as the ones you don't say. Your words may not be saying what you want them to. The best safety precaution is to ask her to tell you what she heard in her own words. If the message is the same, then you're pretty safe. If not, try again.

Another rule of thumb is to simply listen. Men are fixers. When a woman complains about a particular situation, she doesn't always want solutions. Sometimes she just wants to be heard and understood. You can even ask her, "Honey, would you like me to help you solve this problem, or is this an occasion when I'm supposed to just listen?" She'll probably laugh and let you know which one she prefers.

COACH COOPER

Everyone likes to be complimented. Learn to notice small things about a girl so that you can offer sincere, specific compliments. What matters is that it's genuine. Try complimenting five women today, and see how it goes. Don't compliment them because you're hoping to get a phone number out of it. Compliment them because it just might make their day. You'll notice that it's easy and you'll feel more confident afterward as well.

Some simple examples when first meeting someone are:

- I really like your dress.
- You have a great smile.
- You have beautiful eyes.

If you've known someone a while, your compliments will be even more meaningful, and you should be able to come up with something that's a little deeper:

- I've noticed you do a great job at making everyone feel like they're part of the group.
- You are really observant. You can always tell when someone's had a rough day and needs a hand. That's really cool.

Compliments work most of the time, but the truth is that looks matter, and complimenting an attractive woman can have the opposite effect. Some girls get complimented on their looks all the time, both verbally and nonverbally. They may appreciate the compliment, but they probably don't want to date a guy who is intimidated by them or only cares about what's on the outside. Walking up and telling her she's beautiful says that you're intimidated, like every other guy, and you're hoping to win her over with compliments, like every other guy. One of the principles of attraction is to be the exception, and unfortunately beautiful women often date jerks because those guys become the exception by treating them like garbage.

So, how do you talk to a beautiful girl without being a jerk? The same way you would talk to any girl. Be yourself—not your reserved, play-it-safe self—and if you want to give her a compliment, make sure it doesn't have to do with her looks. If you see the girl below the surface and she can tell you're not intimidated by her,

"A man once told me to walk with the Lord. I'd rather walk with the bases loaded."
—Ken Singleton[68]

she'll lower her shields and you can find out if she's the type of girl you want to date.

Here's a fun tip: if you notice a gorgeous girl with food on her face or something hanging from her nose, don't be afraid to discreetly point it out to her. She'll appreciate it and know that you're not intimidated. Chances are, no one else has told her because they're afraid of creating an awkward moment. Remember, be the exception.

STATS

- Blind dates are the most common way for Koreans to find a spouse.[69]

- Only about 10 percent of people who leave their marriage for an affair actually end up happily ever after with the person who caused the breakup.[70]
- There are eighty-six unmarried men for every one hundred unmarried women in the United States.[71]
- New York City has a higher single woman to single man ratio than any other city in the United States.[72]

ASSIGNMENTS

First Base: Compliment her on something specific.
Second Base: Thank her in front of other people.
Third Base: Learn to speak in soft tones to her.
Home Run: Give her a list of all the reasons you think she's awesome. You can put them in a jar and allow her to open one each day.

A LEAGUE OF THEIR OWN

The best thing a girl can do when a guy compliments her is to say, "Thanks!" When a guy says he likes a girl's dress, she tends to say, "What? This old rag?" That will discourage him from complimenting you again, and it's a back-handed way of telling him he's wrong. He's trying to think of something nice to say, so help him out by extending the conversation and saying, "Thanks! I saw something like it in a movie a couple of months ago and I really liked it. What kinds of movies do you like to watch?"

You can also *give* compliments. Guys don't exist to tell you how awesome you are. Here's a tip: compliment a guy on a behavior you like and he'll be sure to repeat it. "I really love that you just washed those dishes, even though they were your roommates." He'll learn that you appreciate his kindness and housekeeping abilities. Be sure to compliment him on his qualities, not just his looks or clothes.

Chapter 13

CATCHER

COURTING AND DATE IDEAS

Women want to be pursued and courted. They want to brag to their girlfriends about how awesome and devoted you are. They compare stories about their dates and how they were proposed to. They want their friends to see how smart they were to snag the best guy out there.

When you're ready to run to the next base and stick with one girl to court, it's not about The Game anymore; it's about the girl. Elder Richard G. Scott said, "When you find you are developing interest in a young woman, show her that you are an exceptional person that she would find interesting to know better. Take her to places that are worthwhile. Show some ingenuity. If you want to have a wonderful wife, you need to have her see you as a wonderful man and prospective husband."[75]

Sure, you could just ask her out. That's perfectly fine and certainly works, but why not do something special? If she ends up marrying you, she'll be able to share the story for the rest of her life. If she doesn't marry you, you can bet she's never going to forget you and will measure all future beaus against you for many years to come.

There is an art to asking a girl out on a date. Be creative. Even if she says no, the next guy who asks her out will have a hard act to follow. Speaking of saying no, if she shuts you down, she's ultimately doing you a favor because you won't be wasting time and money on her without a getting return on your investment. With every no you get, you're one girl closer to getting a yes.

I had a roommate in college who said yes to all the guys who asked her out (and there were many) simply because she wanted to go out to dinner for free or see a movie for free. She admitted that she wasn't interested in any of them romantically, so I always felt sorry for them for spending their hard-earned money on her. Wouldn't you rather a girl be honest with you up front? Instead of being heartbroken and depressed, thank her and move on. I know, easier said than done.

There is nothing wrong with spending no money on a date. There are plenty of things to do for free. In fact, it takes more creativity, and the girl will be impressed. By the way, don't go to a movie on your first date. You can't learn much about each other while sitting in the dark. One of the easiest first dates is going to one of those self-serve frozen yogurt places. It's kind of like the Mormon version of asking a girl out for a drink.

Don't mention a kiss at the end of the first date. The girl is wondering if you're going to try, and the stress really builds when you're standing on the doorstep at the end of the night. One way to reduce the tension is to jokingly say to her, "Don't worry; I don't kiss on the first date."

Girls interpret a guy who kisses on the first date as a player or someone who probably does it with every girl. A kiss should be special. Girls are often hopeless romantics. They want to be special to you.

COACH COOPER

DATES

Women want to feel feminine. The more you're a man, the more feminine they will feel and the more attraction they'll feel toward you. Whether they admit it or not, they probably want you to open the door for them, lead them, and pay for the date.

Do:

- Show up on time, looking good.
- Open the door for her. All of them.
- Have a clean car.
- Get to know her and have a good time.

- Plan a short date. If you do something fun and short, then drop her off, she'll be left wanting more. Once my friends and I figured this out, we never planned long first dates again. It's better to end wanting to spend more time with each other than being bored with each other.
- Pay for the date, especially if you invited her. Some guys will say you shouldn't have to pay because it's unequal for you to have to ask her out, plan the night's entertainment, pick her up, and pay for the date. What has she done? Smile and look pretty? They make a good point, but if you want to be a man and make her feel like a woman, pay for the date. Later on, in the relationship phase, I think it's attractive when a woman wants to plan dates and pay for certain things. It shows she's committed and wants to be an equal partner in the relationship.
- Try hanging out with some friends before the date, just so that you're in a talkative and fun mood. If you haven't talked to a soul all day leading up to your date, it may cost you some awkward conversation before you get into a fun and playful state of mind.

Don't:

- Don't pick her up and ask her what she wants to do. You asked her out, so you need to think of a good activity.
- Don't sit across the table from her at a restaurant. It's not a huge deal, but you'll both feel more comfortable sitting next to each other, and it'll likely be different from what she was expecting. You're not stuck staring at each other, and you're both looking at the same things so you'll have more to talk about. Give it a try and see what you think.
- Don't make it too formal. If you're both uncomfortable, fix it.
- Don't be afraid of a little physical contact. If you're uncomfortable getting close to her, she'll feel it. Be playful and build comfort throughout the date.
- Don't kiss on the first date.

CREATE A TIME WARP

Another tip for dates, especially first dates, is to bounce around several locations during the date. For example, you pick her up at her place, go to a music event, walk to a nearby frozen yogurt place afterward, and then take her home. Moving to different locations on the same date makes it feel like you've spent more time together than you really have. She'll have memories with you going to a concert, walking around town, eating frozen yogurt, and talking in your car. The date may only last a couple hours, but she'll feel like she's spent the equivalent of two or three dates with you because you've created memories in different places.

DATE IDEAS

One of my favorite things to do is find local events in the area. I could take a date to a concert or a special event at a museum. It's fun, memorable, and different. Here are some date ideas:

- Go for a walk.
- Make hot chocolate.
- Go to the park.
- Play Frisbee golf.
- Make a pizza.
- See a concert.
- Do a service project.
- Go to the zoo.
- Visit a bookstore.
- Go to a museum.
- Go sledding.
- Build a sandcastle.
- Fly kites.

- Play tennis.
- Paint something.
- Go shooting.
- Play a board game.
- See a comedy show.
- Build a campfire and make s'mores with friends.
- Make paper airplanes and throw them off something high up.
- Build a snowman.
- Go for a hike.
- Play a game of golf or go to a driving range.
- Visit a planetarium.
- Go to dinner and a movie.
- Rent a tandem bike and go for a ride.
- Get a couple of scooters and go for a ride.
- Go rock climbing.
- Go for a run.
- Cook something.
- Go to a roller disco.
- Go dancing.

HOLD ON

Holding on to things that are meaningful to you and your special lady can be a sweet gesture and mean a lot to her. It's a low-risk investment in the future that will pay off if the two of you get married. If you don't, there's no loss.

Here's what I recommend: When I go out with someone and I see the potential for a serious relationship, I'll start to hold on to things from our dates (movie ticket stubs, notes you pass to each other). You can use those items later on as part of a creative birthday present or even a proposal. Those little knick-knacks can make the experience more meaningful, because it shows you thought she was special right from the beginning, which is true. If there's a breakup (which there will be for every girl you date except one), you can throw it all out and start holding onto things the next time you find a girl who might be the one.

STATS

- The term *chivalry* is from the Latin word *caballus*, meaning "pack-horse" and is related to the word *cavalier*.
- A 2013 MSN survey found that nearly two-thirds of women thirty-five and younger say they offer to pay for dates, but 39 percent hope the guy will turn down the offer and 44 percent get annoyed if he lets her pay.[76]
- One study found that most men believe they are supposed to pay for dates, and a fair number of women let them, but nearly half of men say they'd dump a woman who never offered to help pay.[77]

ASSIGNMENTS

First Base: Plan five creative, free dates.

Second Base: Choose one of your ideas and go on a date.

Third Base: Thank her for the date. Send her a text within twenty-four hours.

Home Run: If the date went well, choose one of your other ideas and ask her out on a second date.

A LEAGUE OF THEIR OWN

A guy had been dating a girl he really liked. One day, when she was in the other room, he looked at her cell phone and found his name next to a note that said, "Free lunch." That's terrible! There were some roommates who had a whiteboard where they kept track of which one scored the most free stuff during the week on dates. That's awful! Girls, don't be so cruel. These guys are trying really hard to get to know you and find true love. Be kind, honest, and upfront about how you feel.

Chapter 14

THE FANS

SCORING POINTS WITH HER FRIENDS

The definition of a true baseball fan is an individual who has the unique ability to sit five hundred feet from home plate and see better than the umpire who's five feet from the plate. Sometimes it's hard to see what a girl is really like when you're blinded by love. Your friends know you and want to protect you from the wrong girl. Ask for their opinions and listen to them if you truly trust their judgment.

This advice applies to girls and their friends about you too. If you want to score more points with your girl, you need to get in with her best friend. Notice I didn't say, "Get it on with her best friend." A cardinal rule of dating is to *never* date your girlfriend's friends after you break up. It's a double betrayal. They are off limits. There are plenty more fish in the sea for you to try, so move on to different waters.

Just like your buddies are protective of you, the friends of the girl you're dating will be watching your every move to see if you're the real deal. They can spot a phony and will warn her. If you treat them well, they will line up to join your fan club.

It's also important how you treat your girlfriend in front of your friends. Do you make fun of her to get a few cheap laughs from your buddies? Do you build her up and brag to everyone how wonderful she is? She needs to feel safe around you.

A word of caution: she also needs to know her friends are safe around you and not going to be hit on by you. I dated a guy who often asked about my girlfriends. I felt so betrayed when I found out he had gone over to one of their houses to hang out without me. Of course, he said it was entirely innocent, but that was a serious red flag that made me realize I couldn't trust him. Without trust, you have no relationship.

COACH COOPER

WOMEN WANT POTENTIAL, NOT PORSCHES

You may have heard that women are attracted to money and power. You also may use that as an excuse for why it's hard to attract women. The truth is, that's just not true. Researchers have asked men and women what they're looking for in a partner, and guess what? They don't say money and power. Women say they want a guy who is fun, confident, nice, and attractive and who they can laugh with and who understands them.[80]

Still not convinced? Think of it this way. Women don't usually marry wealthy, powerful men. Very few guys become wealthy and powerful until later in life, but women *do* want a strong man who is a provider. In their dating years, women become experts at judging a man's *potential*. They're not looking for a young guy who is already wealthy and powerful, although that would be great for them. They're looking for a man with potential. That's why women are attracted to men who are leaders, have ambition, and have goals. If you're not the leader of a group of friends, a club, or anything, it would serve you well to either become one or begin to develop leadership characteristics. If you have no hopes, dreams, or ambitions and are happy working a boring job and playing videogames after work, it's time to look for a higher calling in life. Why should a woman want to be a part of your life if you're not going anywhere? If you come across as lazy, she'll wonder if you'll get fired from a job later in life and she'll have to take care of money issues. That's not attractive.

STATS

- The average adult male has about 50 percent more muscle mass and 50 percent less body fat than the average adult female.[81]

- According to the 2010 US Census Bureau, men received 25 percent fewer college degrees than women.[82]
- A study at the University of Michigan found proof that women drivers are more likely to be involved in an accident. After researching 6.5 million car crashes, they also discovered that women have a tougher time negotiating crossroads, T-junctions, and slip roads.[83]
- A study at Snap Interactive revealed that a man who sends a message to a woman his own age on a dating web site has a 4 percent likelihood of receiving a response; a woman who sends a message to a man her own age has a 17.5 percent likelihood of a reply.[84]

ASSIGNMENTS

First Base: Ask your friends how they feel about the girl you're dating.

Second Base: Ask your girlfriend if you can meet her friends.

Third Base: Do something nice for your girlfriend and her friends.

Home Run: Plan a girls' night for your girlfriend and her friends, letting her know that you recognize their time together is important.

A LEAGUE OF THEIR OWN

Use the same advice I just gave the guys: ask your girlfriends how they feel about the guy you're dating. Really listen to their concerns, if they have any. When hormones and romance are flying, it's difficult to see the difference between reality and fantasy.

It's hard to see his flaws when you're so infatuated by his strengths. I'm not saying to look for weaknesses, but don't ignore them. No guy is ever going to be perfect, but you have to decide what weaknesses you're willing to live with for the rest of your life.

We girls are pretty quick to fall in love. We love the idea of being in love and readily gloss over flaws that could be potential problems. The quality of the man *will* affect the quality of the rest of your life. Choose wisely.

Chapter 15

READING *the* SIGNS

BREAKUPS AND THE FRIEND ZONE

You're probably going to have your heart broken at least once before you get married. It hurts. A lot. It's one of the reasons why finding Mrs. Right is so wonderful. In this chapter, we're going to talk about ending a romance before it has even started (the friend zone), as well as ending an actual romantic relationship. The goal is to learn from the ending relationship so that the next one is better. If you're not learning and improving after each relationship, then you're just suffering in pain for no reason, and you're doomed to repeat the same mistakes that may have been the cause for the breakup. There should never be begging or whining. Leave like a man and then become a better one.

One of my sons had been dating a great girl in high school, but he could feel it ending. He felt her begin to distance herself from him, and he knew "the talk" was coming. He wanted to keep dating her, but he was also getting ready to leave on his mission, so he knew it would be better to end it, but on good terms.

He was really smart and had prepared ahead of time what he wanted to say when "the talk" finally came. He thanked her for the time they had together and expressed appreciation for all of the things he had learned because of her. He assured her that he would always remember their time together fondly and wished her the best for her future. He meant it too.

It's always going to be awkward the next time you see her, but if you end on good terms and act like a gentleman, it won't be so bad.

Face it, you're either going to marry the girl you're dating or break up with her. There are only two possible outcomes. Each relationship you have has the potential to ultimately make you a better husband. So when they end, whether by you or the girl, make sure you have learned healthy patterns of behavior and thank her for making you a better man. Mean it when you say it.

Finally, be a man and just end it. If you just quit answering her calls, texts, or emails, then she's going to be hurt and angry. You'll be the classless jerk who treated her badly. Don't let it just fizzle into nothingness, because she'll wonder what happened. End every relationship on good terms. Don't be her shoulder to cry on. You can't be her ex and her support system. That's what her friends are for. Let her move on. Don't lie about why you want to break up, and *never* text your breakup. Also, you don't know how she's going to react, so don't do it in public where she might cry or humiliate both of you.

Here are some things *not* to say:

- "It's not you. It's me." (She knows that's ridiculous.)
- "Let's just be friends." (She might've been planning your wedding in her mind, so it's too painful for her to be your buddy now.)
- "We can still be kissing buddies." (That's just wrong.)
- "I'm seeing someone else." (She'll feel betrayed.)

Kinder ways to explain it (provided they're true for you):

- "I'm not ready to have a serious relationship right now."
- "We're arguing more than we're having fun, and we both deserve better than that in a relationship."
- "You cheated on me, and I can't accept that."
- "I've been praying about us, and I don't think we're supposed to be together."

COACH COOPER

From time to time, you may find yourself being pursued by a girl you're not interested in. Maybe she sends you texts all the time. Maybe she always seems to be around. Maybe she actually asks you out. If you think you might be interested, that's great. Why not give it a chance? But if you're absolutely positive a relationship with her is less likely than you shaving with a cheese grater, you're in a tough situation.

You can't just ignore her, because that's rude. You definitely can't be mean to her or hurt her feelings, because you're not a jerk. I've found that the best course of action is to simply tell her that you're interested in someone else.

Can men and women be "just friends"? Nope. If a guy and a girl become good friends, have fun spending time with each other, and have a lot in common, why wouldn't they want to be more than friends?

If you're trying to get out of the friend zone or handle a breakup, my advice is the same for both circumstances. First off, if you're about to get dumped, you can probably feel it coming. Let it end on a good note where you act like a gentleman. That will make things easier later on.

The next step, disappear and transform. You need to leave for a while. Don't be the guy that keeps hanging around and never makes a move. Whether disappearing means hanging out with different people or going to different places, it's necessary, because a gradual change won't be as noticeable.

Once you're gone, you need to make some changes. Become a better you, date other people, find a new hobby, and forget about her. It's over.

Last step, when you see your ex (or the girl who had you in the friend zone), you should be a different person, new and improved. If you did all this half-heartedly just because you were trying to win her back, she'll probably be able to see right through it. If you were truly able to forget about her, transform, and date other people, you will probably realize you have moved on and found someone better for the new you.

A little tip on physical contact: don't be afraid to give her a hug when you see her again, but when you do hug her, pat her on the back a few times. Women can feel what is conveyed through different hugs, and a hug with a pat or two on the back is a hug between friends. This shows that you're no longer physically attracted, which is an important change from how things used to be.

STATS

- Most women walking down the aisle smile; men frown. According to the scientists, this is due to nervousness; women hide it behind the smile, and men hide it behind severity.[87]
- Happiness of a girl is in inverse relationship with her beauty. Statistics show that the most beautiful girls tend to be unhappy after twenty-five years.[88]
- According to a 2008 study in the *Proceedings of the National Academy of Science*, genetics may play a role in the fact that some men have a harder time with commitment. Men without the "promiscuity gene," an estimated 60 percent of the population, are more likely to marry.[89]

ASSIGNMENTS

First Base: Write a list of the things you have learned from your relationship that has ended.

Second Base: Ask yourself and the Lord what you need to do to improve yourself for the next relationship.

Third Base: Choose at least one thing you need to work on to be a better you.

Home Run: Don't be afraid to get hurt again. Start dating other girls.

A LEAGUE OF THEIR OWN

All of the advice above is meant for you too. You can't force or convince someone to love you. If he's ready to move on, let him go. Don't become a lifeless puddle or a crazy stalker. You also shouldn't waste your tears or hours of thinking about what could have been or should have been. The fact that you didn't marry him means there is someone even better out there for you. Whether he broke your heart or you broke his, take time to consider what worked and what didn't so you can learn from the relationship.

Chapter 16

BATTING AVERAGE

PERSISTENCE PAYS OFF

Don't give up. Persistence pays off. You may have the righteous desire to be married right now, but it's simply not happening the way you want it to. Don't give up trying to find her. She's out there somewhere.

Don't miss out on a blessing because it isn't packaged the way you expect. When our lives don't go according to our plans, we often fail to see the Lord's hand in the change. I have a son who has always worried that he needs to be in the right place at the right time in order for the Lord to work through him. If you're doing what you're supposed to be doing, the Lord will place you where He needs you.

President Gordon B. Hinckley assured us, "God is weaving his tapestry according to his own grand design. All flesh is in his hands. It is not our prerogative to counsel him. It is our responsibility and our opportunity to be at peace in our minds and in our hearts, and to know that he is God, that this is his work, and that he will not permit it to fail."[92]

Elder Richard G. Scott said, "When your life complies with the will of the Lord and is in harmony with His teachings, the Holy Ghost is your companion in need. You will be able to be inspired by the Lord to know what to do. When needed, your efforts will be fortified with divine power. You can be protected and strengthened to do what alone would be impossible."[93] Isn't that an awesome promise?

If you're not finding Mrs. Right in the usual places, try some different ones. Here are a few ideas:

- Take some fun classes at your local community center.
- Go to the museum, library, or park.
- Take a class at the local college

- Surf forums or message boards about your favorite hobbies or ones you'd like to learn more about.
- Play an instrument in a local band or orchestra that takes you places.
- Join a gym.
- See what upcoming events are happening in your town and attend.
- Volunteer to help backstage at a stage performance.
- Team up with others on a local service project.
- Get off your couch and attend a festival, expo, or conference where people are passionate about their work or hobbies.

I have a beautiful niece who is constantly being pursued by suitors. I recently asked her boyfriend how he won her over, and he admitted he had to battle the competition. Actually, his real words were, "I had to assert myself as the alpha male." He asked her what it was that finally earned her heart, and she simply said, "You were more persistent."

COACH COOPER

Here are some places you can meet girls:

- Your local singles ward, stake activities, and conferences
- Spin cycling classes
- Hip-hop dance classes
- Yoga classes
- Service projects
- Grocery stores

The truth is, you can meet girls almost anywhere. If you don't live in an area where there is a large population of LDS women, things get a little more complicated. When it comes down to it, you just need to look at your priorities. Is your desire to find the right woman great enough that you're willing to go to Church activities for singles? Or try online dating? Or move to a different state? Take a hard look at what you really want in life and it will become more obvious what you need to do to get there.

STATS

- Most often, men start a conversation and women finish it.[94]
- According to the *Los Angeles Times,* men are the product of an X and a Y chromosome. Their maleness is in the Y chromosome. However, Y is usually the inactive genes. Therefore, men's genetic instructions are found in one chromosome, the

X. Women, on the other hand, have more genetic instructions since they are the product of two X chromosomes.[95]

- Studies about laughter reveal that men enjoy shallow slapstick humor more than women. [96]
- According to *Nature*, the time difference between men's and women's speed in the 100-meter run has been shrinking. If the time difference continues to shrink as it has been throughout the 1900s, by 2156, women will be faster than men, at least in the 100-meter run.[97]

ASSIGNMENTS

First Base: Sign up for a community class.

Second Base: Be willing to go on a blind date.

Third Base: Sign up for an LDS singles conference outside your regular area.

Home Run: Throw a party for other singles to get to know each other.

A LEAGUE OF THEIR OWN

Sadly, some girls don't feel complete unless they have a boyfriend. Some girls feel like they can't start living their "real" life until they're married. What if they never get married? I've got some startling news for you: your "real" life has already started. What kind of a life do you want to have *now?*

As members of the Church, we all desire a family of our own and the white picket fence that proves we're living happily ever after. The truth is, you don't know the Lord's timing for you when it comes to marriage and children, so don't put your life on hold while you wait for those wonderful blessings to come. Focus on your goals in all areas of your life and work toward them now.

My oldest sister dated a lot, but it wasn't until she was in her thirties that she finally found Mr. Right. She wondered if she would ever find him and was frustrated with the Lord's timing. She kept working on her other goals and decided that she needed to create a happy life as a single woman rather than postpone happiness. The marriage and babies came eventually, but she learned an important lesson: life is happening now, so don't waste a minute of it.

Chapter 17

SPRING TRAINING

COULD SHE BE THE ONE FOR YOU?

Studies show that people date more in the spring when the warmer weather outside melts snow and hearts. The reason for dating a girl exclusively is to learn more about her with the end goal of determining whether she is the best match for you to marry. As you date, you may discover certain qualities or values that are "deal breakers." That's helpful information. It's much better to find out sooner rather than later.

I'm often amazed at young couples who marry without really knowing each other. I'm a romantic at heart, so I appreciate the idea of love at first sight and being swept off your feet. I'm also realistic enough to know that there are some conversations that absolutely must be had before a ring goes on anyone's finger. There are some basic ones, like:

- What do you want out of life?
- What are your expectations in marriage?
- What do you see yourself doing in ten years? Twenty? Thirty?

- Do you want to have children? How many?
- What kind of career do you want to have?

Here are a few more good ones to get you started:

- How much debt do you consider to be acceptable?
- Would you stay married if your spouse were in a terrible car accident and became disfigured?
- If your spouse were in a coma, would you pull the plug?
- What would you do if your boss told you to do something illegal or immoral, or you'd be fired?
- What do you expect your spouse to do, be, and have?
- If you had to choose one over the other, would you choose freedom or security?
- What are the items on your bucket list?
- If your country drafted you, would you serve in the military or run to another country?
- Should children be spanked?
- How do you feel about credit cards?
- How do you feel about the death penalty?
- Are you going to teach your children about Santa and the Easter Bunny?
- Are you a saver or a spender?
- How do you feel about kissing in public?
- What is your greatest fear?
- Which do you feel is better for your future children: public school, private school, or homeschool?
- Are there men's jobs and women's jobs?
- If you had to kill a family member in order to save the country from some kind of terrible destruction, would you do it?

- How do you feel about breastfeeding in public?
- What would cause you to get a divorce?
- Which political party do you feel best represents your economic and social values?
- How much money should you always keep in an emergency fund?

Before you propose to a girl, there is one more really important question to ask:

- I know you want to get married, but why do you want to marry *me*?

COACH COOPER

When you begin dating, it's important to keep it playful and fun while getting to know her. Here are a couple of silly conversations you can have during the early stages of dating someone

THE FIVE-QUESTIONS GAME (ROUND ONE)

This game is fun, short, and great for making some kind of wager beforehand, like the loser has to tell an embarrassing story. Here's an example:

You: Have you ever played the five-questions game?

Her: I don't think so. What is it?

You: I will ask you five questions. To win, you have to answer incorrectly each time. For example, I ask what day of the week it is. Today is Monday, so you have to say any day but Monday, like Thursday. Got it?

Her: Seems simple enough.

Now you set the stakes, which could be dinner, a movie, or an embarrassing story.

You: Question one: What city are we in?

Her: London.

You: What is your name?

Her: Katherine.

You: What color is that wall over there?

Her: Bright pink.

You: Okay . . . wait how many questions was that?

Her: Sneaky. We're on question eight.

You: You got me. But you've played this game before, haven't you?

Her: No, I never have.

You: Got you on question five.

This will put a smile on her face, and you can have so much fun with it. Now, here's a follow-up game you can play with the same girl, maybe later that same night.

THE FIVE-QUESTIONS GAME (ROUND TWO)

You: Want a second chance at that questions game we played earlier?

Her: Okay, but I don't think you'll be able to trick me again.

You: This one's a little different. It's still five questions, but you have to say the right answer this time.

Her: Deal.

You: First, let me see one of your hands.

Take her by the hand and hold her hand as you ask the following questions.

You: Question one: What color is my shirt?

Her: Blue.

You: Question two: Did you brush your teeth today?

Her: Yes, I did.

You: Where were you born?

Her: Virginia.

You: What day of the week is it?

Her: Friday.

With your free hand, take your finger and move it as close to her nose as you possibly can without actually touching her.

You: Last question: Am I touching you?

Her: Nope.

Lift up your other hand, which is still holding her hand, to reveal that she has lost again.

You might not always win at this game, so be careful what you're betting. It's not a guaranteed win.

STATS

- Women have a one-in-eight chance for a second date if they have not heard from the guy within twenty-four hours of their first date.[101]
- Women have fifteen minutes to make a first impression on a man. Men have about an hour to make a first impression.[102]

ASSIGNMENTS

First Base: Ask yourself questions about what you really value in life.

Second Base: Ask your girlfriend the same questions and really listen.

Third Base: Search online for more compatibility questions to ask to help evaluate if you're right for each other.

Home Run: Find out what items are on her bucket list and do one with her.

A LEAGUE OF THEIR OWN

"Another bride sighed blissfully on her wedding day, 'Mom, I'm at the end of all my troubles!' 'Yes,' replied her mother, 'but at which end?' "[103]

We girls love the notion of a knight in shining armor who rescues us from our troubles. We love the stories that end with the princess living happily ever after with her handsome prince. The reality is that no matter how amazing your prince is, you *will* have challenges and problems in your life.

You'll never truly know someone until after you've married him, so how can you possibly make an informed decision? Share lots of different kinds of experiences with your boyfriend and see how he reacts in various environments. Ask each other lots of questions that will reveal each other's values. What you're looking for is how he solves problems and resolves conflicts. Does he yell like a child having a tantrum? Does he approach a crisis with a calm head? Is he kind when he's hurt? Is he mean when he's sick? If your man is still Christlike when under pressure, then you've got yourself a real keeper. Now, ask those same questions about yourself.

Chapter 18

SEMI-PRO

SCORING THE FIRST KISS

Semi-pro is what every young baseball player strives for. In The Game, it's when you go from dating someone you like to entering a relationship, which includes such perks as holding hands and kissing. Knowing when the girl is ready to take that leap with you can be tricky.

Elder Holland gives a great sports analogy that is perfectly appropriate for this book's theme. He said,

> In almost all athletic contests of which I know, there are lines drawn on the floor or the field within which every participant must stay in order to compete. Well, the Lord has drawn lines of worthiness. . . . We need young men who are already on the team to stay on it and stop dribbling out of bounds just when we need you to get into the game and play your hearts out! And with this game on the line, what this coach is telling you is that to play in this match, some of you have to be more morally clean than you now are. In this battle between good and evil, you cannot play for the Adversary whenever temptation comes along and then

> expect to suit up for the Savior at temple and mission time as if nothing has happened.[106]

You have probably all heard the parable about the wagon drivers who were asked how close they could drive to a cliff's edge. While other drivers boasted about how close they could get without falling off the ledge, one man said he would never put his wagon in jeopardy by riding so close.[107] Guys, don't ask how far you can go with a girl and to still be temple worthy. Let there be no question about your worthiness. Stay far away from the edge.

How do you stay far away from the edge? First, you need to draw your own line *before* you're in the heat of the moment with your girl. Don't compromise or justify your standards based on the moment. Your line should be in the same place as the Lord's.

Now, the Lord never told you to wait until you're kneeling at the altar before you have your first kiss. So go for it. However, the Lord has set clear boundaries for expressions of affection that go beyond kissing. When you reach a certain level of comfort with physical affection, it's difficult to go backward. Once you've gone to kissing, you will find it difficult to be happy with just holding hands. Be firm on your standards. Think with your brain, not your hormones.

Here's something that makes a distinction between men and women. A girl is perfectly content to kiss for hours, whereas a guy is already thinking about more. I hate it when a guy gets a girl pregnant and says, "Well, one thing led to another." There are *many* moments between kissing and going all the way when you can stop. I'm not going to say it's easy, but you have to stop. That one moment of pleasure can destroy both of your lives.

Elder Jeffrey R. Holland shared,

> Someone said once that true love must include the idea of permanence. True love endures. But lust changes as quickly as it can turn a pornographic page or glance at yet another potential object for gratification walking by. True love we are absolutely giddy about. We shout it from the house tops. But lust is

> characterized by shame and stealth and is almost pathologically clandestine—the later and darker the hour, the better, with a double-bolted door just in case. Love comes with open hands and open heart. Lust comes with only an open appetite.[108]

The only real control is self-control. The Church has established guidelines to help you, but there is no law of chastity ninja who will pop out of the couch cushions to stop you in the heat of the moment. Think about *who* she is, not *what* she is.

Kissing is fun. I highly recommend it. Just be smart about it.

COACH COOPER

If physical contact is difficult for you and you're not sure when a girl is okay with you touching her, I understand. In high school, I sat through an entire movie with a girl I had a crush on, only to find out months later that she had her arm sitting on my armrest, palm up, fingers open, waiting the whole movie for me to hold her hand.

On another occasion, years later, I was on a date with a different girl and this girl got tired of my inability to recognize her signals. She said she wanted to compare hand sizes to see how big my hand was. As our hands were pressed together, the cogs in my mind slowly clicked into place. I finally realized this must mean she wanted me to hold her hand.

THE KISS CLOSE

Going for a first kiss can be nerve wracking. If it isn't, then maybe you're not that attracted to her in the first place and a kiss is not in the lineup. We talked about IOIs earlier; there are several indicators to look for that will tell you if she would like to be kissed.

Touch her hair: If you can run your hand through her hair and she doesn't pull away at all, you can be pretty sure she's ready for a kiss. This is pretty easy. If the two of you are sitting next to each other, you're close enough to brush your hand through her hair and comment on how nice it is.

Physical proximity: You can judge, based on body position, how comfortable your date is with your physical touch. If you're sitting close together, whispering in each other's ears, and she's leaning in as you're talking, these are all good signs. If she hesitates or leans back, she's not quite ready.

Long eye contact: Take close physical proximity and a lull in conversation and add long eye contact. You can bet this is the moment she is hoping you'll lean in to kiss her. That or she's thinking you're a terrible conversationalist.

Excited Anticipation: If a girl is locking eyes with you with an expression like the one she gets toward the end of one of her

favorite chick flicks or (if she's a sports person) when her team is mere feet away from a game-winning goal, she might want you to kiss her.

Plays with her lips: A girl might play with her lips in several ways. She may bite, touch, pinch, or lick her lips or apply lip balm. She is trying to draw your attention to her lips, and she also doesn't want her lips to be dry for that magic moment.

Triangular gazing: This is a technique where you move your gaze from a woman's left eye, to her right eye, to her lips, and back to her eyes in a triangular movement. As your gaze is shifting from her eyes to her lips, you're communicating that you want to kiss her. If she begins to gaze at your lips as well, this is the go-ahead. She wants you to kiss her. Act fast before she wonders why you're hesitating.

Eager eyes: Eyes can tell you almost anything. If your girl's eyes seem to shine with excitement or eagerness when she looks into yours and her head is slightly tilted, she is anticipating a kiss.

STATS

- Signs that a woman is not interested in her date include avoiding eye contact, faking a smile, leaning away, answering in monosyllables, sagging her shoulders, looking at her watch, or staring blankly.
- Some of the worst places to go on a first date include fast-food restaurants, your parents' house, a party where your ex will be, or streets for window-shopping.
- Dating specialists suggest that if a woman doesn't return a call after two messages, she is not interested.[109]
- If a woman offers to pay for everything, chances are she isn't that into the date.

ASSIGNMENTS

First Base: Touch her elbow three times during your date.

Second Base: Plan an activity that requires you to touch your date, such as a dance class, ice-skating, or three-legged soccer.

Third Base: Hold her hand.

Home Run: Go for the kiss.

A LEAGUE OF THEIR OWN

Guys are thinking about that good-night kiss long before the date even begins. While you're trying to decide what to wear on the date, he's trying hard not to imagine you taking it off. Guys have been created by a loving Heavenly Father to be attracted to women, so don't be so insulted that he's not necessarily thinking about your testimony.

You have no idea the effect you have on guys. I remember the day I started to catch on. When I was in middle school, I sat next to a guy I thought was really attractive. I wore a skirt to school one day, and I remember how the guy stared at me for what seemed like an awkward eternity. Finally, he said, "Wow! Look at those legs." I had no idea what he was talking about. I mean, legs? I remember going home at the end of the school day and staring at my legs in a full-length mirror to see what was wrong with them.

Their hormones make them go crazy thinking about you. Help them to think pure thoughts by dressing modestly. Don't tease them by trying to act like a sexy supermodel. I have four boys and they *all* agree that they appreciate it more when you help them be morally clean. They admire you way more when you dress modestly and respect your own body. The world needs you to be good and kind and clean and true.

Chapter 19

PEANUTS *and* CRACKER JACKS

KINDNESS IN A NUTSHELL

This chapter should probably be the largest one because the success of a relationship is truly determined by kindness. You're cool? Great! You're sexy? Awesome! You're rich? Even better! But if you're a jerk, it's game over. Make sure when you show your true colors, they're colors your girl will admire.

I dated a guy in college who showed his true colors one day when I was sick, and they were colors to be admired. I lived in a "Spanish House" at BYU where all of the girls were learning the language and were required to only speak Spanish when in the home. My boyfriend lived in the "Arabic House," and we were in the same international ward on campus. It was a great experience.

I got the flu and ended up sick in bed for days. My boyfriend was worried and called to let me know he was thinking of me. He even asked me if there was anything he could do for me. I said, "No, don't worry. I'm fine." I wasn't. People rarely are when they say that.

They sometimes want you to read their mind, and then they get mad when you can't

When your girl says she doesn't need help, offer to help her again. But if she really presses, then respect her wishes and back off. When she says nothing is wrong, she may not actually mean it. Sometimes she's just seeing how much you care. I know that's kind of frustrating and confusing. Here's a safe way to handle it. Say, "I know you're fine, but I'd still like to do something for you right now. Is that okay?" She'll most likely melt, and you'll see how she's really doing.

Now, back to the story about my college boyfriend. It was my turn to do some of the cleaning chores in the house, but I could barely lift my head off the pillow. Like a truly kind young man, my boyfriend ignored my weak resistance and came over to the Spanish House. Without telling me he was there, he did all my chores for me: sweeping, mopping, and vacuuming. Then he left. It didn't take long before some of the girls in the house came to my bedroom to visit me and tell me how sweet my boyfriend was. They were so impressed with his kind service. I had no idea he had been serving me and my roommates all day. What impressed me even more was that he didn't call me afterward to brag about what he had done. He scored major points in my eyes that day, as well as in the eyes of the other girls in the house.

Girls want a guy who is macho and manly, but they also want someone who they know will hold their hair back while they throw up in the toilet with morning sickness. That's not exactly a pretty image, and she hopes you'll never have to do that. She just wants to know that you'd be willing to. Common courtesy will go a long way in a relationship. So will the golden rule, "Do unto others as you would have others do unto you."

Whether you treat others with respect or not says more about you than it does about the other person. Be kind to waiters, mailmen, janitors, ticket takers—everyone. Your girl will feel so lucky to be with someone who is truly Christlike rather than have to make excuses to her friends and family about your terrible behavior.

The reason couples have problems can be boiled down to one thing: selfishness. Almost every marital problem I can think of has selfishness at its core. Pornography, finances, and intimate relations, which are three of the biggest relationship issues married couples face, can be condensed into a matter of who is being selfish and unkind.

Over many years, I have watched married couples bicker and fight over the dumbest things. I think it looks ugly. It's one thing to argue over trivial matters, but it's truly astounding when couples do it in front of others. I remember going to a family's house for dinner when I was a young girl and hearing the parents snap at each other over trivial matters all night long in front of all us. I was shocked they would act like that in front of us. Everyone felt uncomfortable just being in their house with them. I swore then that I would never do that.

"It took eight hours, seven and a half to find the heart."
—Steven Earl McCatty on Charlie Finley's heart surgery[110]

It really is the everyday small things that matter most to a woman. Remember, it's the frequent, consistent base hits that ultimately win the game. My brother-in-law always makes sure the car his wife drives has gas in it and is well maintained, because he wants to make sure she's safe. One of the man's roles in family proclamation is to protect.[112] A woman wants to feel safe around you and by you. Be her hero.

Marry someone who is kind. Life is rough, and you simply don't want to spend it with someone who nitpicks over every one of your imperfections. We all have imperfections. Make sure you find someone who can live with yours.

COACH COOPER

BE A NICE GUY WHILE BEING YOURSELF

Women want nice guys but not weak guys. I'm not talking about physical strength at all. I'm talking about being a self-validating man of high social value. Self-validating means he doesn't need other people to compliment him for him to know that he's valuable. A strong man doesn't apologize for existing. He isn't the servant in the relationship, constantly working to meet the woman's every need so that she'll stay with him. I'm not saying that you shouldn't do nice things for a girl. You should! But realize that if you do it because you're trying to buy a girl's time and attention, you might be create the opposite effect and DLV yourself.

Being a nice guy often means you are boring and forgettable. Are you yourself when you go out and talk to women? Your complete self? Or are you a nice guy who doesn't say or do anything out of the ordinary because you don't want to get rejected? A common problem among men (or AFCs) is being boring when talking to women. Like asking lots of questions about her life without ever talking about yourself. If you really think about it, it's all about rejection. Of course rejection hurts. Men sometimes have boring conversations because if they're rejected, they subconsciously feel that they weren't really rejected. After all, the woman never *really* got to know them and they weren't *really* themselves. But they will almost always get rejected that way because they're uninteresting. Why not risk trying harder? Be bold and playful. Talk about what you like. If she's still not interested in the real you, then she's simply not the right girl for you.

What does it mean to be a man? A man places others before himself. I've met a lot of males in their forties and fifties who I wouldn't call men, and I've also met teenagers who could easily be called men. Honoring your priesthood will make you a man, because the priesthood is based on service. Live worthy of the constant companionship of the Spirit. Go to the temple frequently. Do your home teaching.

I know a lot of fathers and Church leaders who tell the young women of the Church to marry a man who is a good home teacher. It is a better indicator of his commitment to live the gospel than whether or not he served a mission. I tend to agree. A man honors his priesthood through service. A man does his home teaching because he has learned to place others before himself. Be the kind of man the woman of your dreams *wants* to be with. Be just as strong in the gospel as you are in society.

STATS

- Studies show that schools, grocery stores, and malls are all good places to flirt because people are more open to meeting others in those places. Poor locations include restaurants and movie theaters.[113]
- Studies show that before a man even speaks a word, the way he stands (whether he is slouching or not) counts for over 80 percent of a woman's first impression of him.[114]
- Mirroring (duplicating the other person's body language) impresses a date because it subtly conveys interest to the other person.

ASSIGNMENTS

First Base: Leave a generous tip when you two go out for dinner and make the restaurant staff feel good about their hard work. Let her see you praise them.

Second Base: Carry in the groceries for her.

Third Base: Before you plop down on the couch to watch TV or play video games, say to her, "I have fifteen minutes. What can I do for you?" You'll score romance points with this question *every* time. Once you begin that pattern of behavior, she'll begin to copy it and ask you the same question.

Home Run: Buy her flowers on a Tuesday or day that isn't a holiday just to let her know you were thinking of her.

A LEAGUE OF THEIR OWN

Many years ago, I was driving with my baby into a grocery store parking lot and noticed a jerk in an expensive sports car quickly grab a spot another driver had been patiently waiting for. The driver shook his fist at the inconsiderate man, who laughed and walked into the store with his female companion. I thought to myself, "How could she be with such a jerk?"

After I finished shopping and loaded up my car, I sat at the opening to the intersection in front of the store, waiting for the string of cars to leave a gap so I could merge into the traffic. Suddenly, a car bumped me from behind, hard. I looked in the rearview mirror and was shocked to see the same jerk from earlier.

He hit my car so hard that it bumped my car up on to the curb and knocked my tire off. As I got out of the car, I saw his female companion just sitting there, refusing to make eye contact with me. He and I exchanged information, and then I had to call a tow truck to take me to the nearest tire store to fix my vehicle. I got my baby out of the car and waited for help while my groceries melted in the trunk. The man laughed and drove off. Later that day, I found out the identification information he had given me was phony.

That woman just sat there and did nothing. How could she be with such a man? Sure, he obviously had a lot of money. That doesn't make it okay to treat people like garbage. Don't *ever* waste one minute with a man like that.

There are plenty of red flags when you're dating that will reveal the kind of man you're with. Pay attention to them. When you find yourself making excuses for his bad behavior, recognize that as one of the red flags. Most people are on their best behavior when dating, so if it's bad now, imagine how terrible it could get after you're married to him. Don't make the mistake of thinking you'll change him. Either he has good character now or he doesn't. The only one who can change him is himself.

Chapter 20

OUTFIELDER

VIDEO GAMES AND GIRLS

Technology is awesome. I get it. I love it too. Why then is this chapter even in this book? Because all of the girlfriends and wives I talked to are concerned about this issue and worried about how it's affecting your relationships. They're worried that you'll get sucked into your devices and never come back. They're worried that you won't know how to communicate with other human life forms and that you'll be the geeky husband and dad who can't utter a coherent sentence anymore.

They're concerned that you haven't learned proper manners, like looking people in the eye when they speak to you or not using your cell phone at the dinner table. They're afraid you're turning into a zombie and can't function without technology. I have a son who would actually curl into the fetal position whenever we would take away his computer. He didn't even know what to do with himself. Women worry. That's what we do.

When my kids were little, they were usually the ones who played in the outfield on their little league teams. They were the ones who were catching butterflies and daydreaming out in the grass while the real game was happening in the infield. You're playing in the outfield in your relationship when you get sucked into your technology to an unhealthy degree.

Video games are fun, but they shouldn't be your life. This is the part where I tell you to cut down the amount of time you spend playing video games. Yeah, I know that's what you heard when parents started to lecture about gaming. The truth is that video games suck hours out of your day and life. And yeah, I know girls play too. Sure, you learn eye-hand coordination skills that will come in handy if you become a drone operator in the military, but you need to make sure you know how to fill your spare time with other activities that will develop meaningful talents, qualities, and relationships as well.

The Word of Wisdom teaches us the importance of moderation in all things (see D&C 89). That applies to gaming, surfing the net, and chatting online. What you're ingesting into your body for hours at a time when you play video games is often violence. Try setting a timer, and then when it goes off, stop playing and move on to a different activity that helps you become the man you truly want to become.

If you struggle with technology addictions, I encourage you to read Elder Bednar's excellent talk from a BYU fireside entitled "Things As They Really Are." In it, he says, "I raise an apostolic voice of warning about the potentially stifling, suffocating, suppressing, and constraining impact of some kinds of cyberspace interactions and experiences upon our souls."[117]

I totally get that a guy has to have playtime with his bros. Once you're married, you need to arrange for "broments," as well as encourage your wife to set aside time for girls' night out. It's healthy for both of you. What will hurt your marriage is if you haven't learned how to manage your time or be disciplined enough to step away from the video games when the lawn needs to be mowed.

Some of your parents and Church leaders are worried that you're living in a 2-D world on your cell phone and missing out on the real world. I'll never forget a Young Women activity I worked many hours planning with the lofty idea that the girls would get to know each other better and create eternal bonds. It was a Christmas dinner where we were supposed to sing Christmas carols from house to house as we enjoyed a different dinner course in each beautifully decorated home on our wintery route. I was shocked when all of the girls arrived at the first house, sat on the couch, and immediately pulled out their cell phones to text other friends. What was even crazier is when we found out that two of the girls were texting each other while they sat right next to each other.

I remember hearing Jason Wright, the author of the fantastic novel *Christmas Jars*, speak at a Time Out for Women session. He held his new iPhone lovingly in his hand and said, "You complete me." He was joking, of course, but I know that some people really do feel more connected to their technology than to real people.

When a girl sees you playing video games, she's asking herself what kind of husband and father you'll be. Girls are always thinking about that. She's worried that she'll end up marrying a boy rather than a man. Sure, there's a time and a place for video games. You're wife might even like to play video games with you every once in a while. I'm just giving you the heads up now that it's not the time when diapers need changing, the lawn needs mowing, or the window blinds need fixing. You want to see a look of resentment on a woman's face? Just play video games or surf the net when she needs your help around the house.

If you've got a video game addiction now, you'd better start weaning yourself off it. There are not many girls out there who are going to want to be second pick after gaming.

COACH COOPER

ONLINE DATING

I was never a fan of online dating in the past, because I lived in areas where there were a lot of LDS girls. Online dating seemed

like a crutch. Wouldn't it be easier to just go outside (and walk around BYU campus, for example) to find girls? That said, if you live in an area where there aren't thousands of attractive and available LDS women, online dating might be a smart move. In my opinion, the phrase *online dating* is misleading. It should be called "online meeting," because you can meet and attract people online, but you can't really date someone online.

In order to better serve you in this book, I tried an experiment. I created an online profile of a fake attractive woman to see what other men would say. About 95 percent of the messages I saw other guys send were a variation of "hi :)" or "You are really pretty. We should chat." The outcome of this experiment was I learned that most men say the same things to attractive women. If you want to stand out, try initiating a conversation by commenting on something she wrote in her profile or something in her picture, like, "You're not a hardcore Harry Potter fan, are you? I don't know how

I feel about you trying to cast spells on me." Whatever you say, just make it interesting and different. Your chances are slim if you only communicate, "You're attractive; please talk to me."

There are a lot of articles online about how to be successful in online dating, and if that's something you want to do, I recommend doing some research beforehand. There are some interesting studies out there. For example, did you know that online dating sites have done all kinds of research into what types of profile pictures draw the most attention? Apparently, the pictures of men that get the most attention from women are the ones where the guy isn't looking directly at the camera. Pictures of guys with animals also receive a lot of clicks by female viewers.[118]

STATS

- 48 percent of men say they want to meet their girlfriend's parents before becoming exclusive. And 35 percent of women said the same.[119]
- 54 percent of daters say they wouldn't date someone with more than $5,000 in credit card debt.[120]
- 22 percent of single women said they secretly searched their date's pockets, drawers, or closets. Women over thirty headed straight for their date's medicine cabinet. 44 percent of single women in their thirties and 38 percent of those in their forties said they'd snooped around for incriminating prescriptions.[121]
- An ourtime.com survey found that 40 percent of Americans approve of spying on a boyfriend or girlfriend if they suspect foul play.[122]

ASSIGNMENTS

First Base: Put down the remote control.

Second Base: Delete games off your cell phone so they won't distract you anymore.

Third Base: Give yourself a time limit for when you play and be disciplined to actually stop playing when the timer goes off.

Home Run: Find a game you can play with your girl that she enjoys or discover a new hobby you can do together.

A LEAGUE OF THEIR OWN

I just got through telling the guys to stop playing video games so much. That being said, you need to ease up a little bit. Maybe

you shop. Maybe they game. We all have different ways of relaxing and having fun. The key is moderation in all things, of course. Have you ever played with him? If not, ask him to find a game he thinks you'll enjoy together.

If you're dating a guy who spends endless hours gaming or watching YouTube videos without stepping into the real world often, you may need to move on to a guy who can handle the real world.

Chapter 21

THE BULLPEN

ARE YOU FATHER MATERIAL?

When dating, men judge the date by how often the girl laughed and if he got a kiss at the end of the night. Women judge the date by considering if it was a good investment toward the future—will he be a good husband and father?

When you're dating, girls watch when you interact with children to see if you're "father material." Remember, girls see the big picture, so they're already analyzing how you will be in ten years or thirty years. She's wondering if you'll teach your son how to play baseball. She's picturing your daughter with her feet on top of your shoes as you teach her to waltz around the living room.

A woman's biological clock starts ticking, and she knows she has a limited number of years to find Mr. Right and begin her family. Biologically, men can father children almost until they die, so their clock never starts ticking. Heavenly Father designed it that way, so don't get angry when your girl starts dreaming about your future family together.

You might be freaking out a little bit here. What if you don't even like children? I promise you that babysitting other people's snotty-nosed rug rats is rather different from holding your own child in your arms. Having children will open up an entire new world to you—a better, more meaningful world. Many men I've talked to say that when they had their own baby is when they finally "woke up."

We don't just automatically become awesome parents who teach our children to read scriptures and pray. We have to start those habits ourselves long before we even have a family of our own. Elder Richard G. Scott revealed, "We become what we want to be by consistently being what we want to become."[124]

Having children definitely changes your relationship. You won't be able to hit the midnight movies spontaneously anymore, but you will be able to feel complete joy, understand Heavenly Father on an entirely new level, and experience pure love like you've never imagined. It sounds like a pretty good trade-off to me.

What if you're in no way near ready to have children? Then don't have sex. Your chances of having a child increase dramatically when you have sex. But what if you're married and you're not ready for children? Then use your brain and plan carefully, realizing that you will never *truly* be ready for children. If we all waited until all our education was finished and we had enough money, then hardly anyone would have children. As a couple, counsel with the Lord on this eternally important matter.

Speaking of parenting, some couples get engaged without ever meeting each other's parents, thinking, "It doesn't matter what they're like because we're in love!" I hate to break it to you, but it's kind of a package deal. Her parents are going to want you to spend Christmas with them. Her siblings are going to be sitting next to you at the Thanksgiving table. They may want to go on vacations with you or even move next door to you. You need to see the whole package before you decide to make it a part of your life forever. You really do marry the family. Make sure you like them, because you'll be dealing with them for the rest of your life.

"If a woman has to choose between catching a fly ball and saving an infant's life, she will choose to save the infant's life without even considering if there are men on base." —Dave Barry[123]

COACH COOPER

Are you good with kids? Are you responsible and a good example? Are you a provider and a protector? Women are way better at taking these things into consideration early on in the dating process. In addition to becoming these things yourself, my advice is to ask yourself if the woman you're interested in will be a good mother. That's probably not on our minds when we first start dating someone. But when you get past being entranced by her beauty, ask yourself these questions: Is she kind? Is she patient? Is she good with kids? Is she happy? Will she be a good teacher? Is she the role model whose example you would want your daughters to follow?

Make sure the girl you're dating is equipped to raise the valiant children you want to have. She will, most likely, spend more time with your children than you will, so her parenting skills should definitely be considered before you get more serious.

STATS

- According to a study in *Evolution and Human Behavior* in 2000, fathers-to-be go through hormone changes: prolactin goes up, and testosterone goes down.[125]
- Studies show that the way dads play with their kids (more rough-housing, more spontaneity, more teasing) can help kids learn better, be more confident, and prepare them for the real world.[126]
- Women spend nearly one year of their lives deciding what to wear.[127]
- Women's hearts beat faster than men's.[128]

ASSIGNMENTS

First Base: Take her to a playground so she can see how playful you are. Swing on the swings and go down the slides.

Second Base: Go on a date where you babysit someone else's kids so she can see you in action. Find a young couple with children and offer to babysit for free while they go to the temple.

Third Base: Volunteer together at a school, Boys and Girls Club, YMCA, Church nursery, or another organization for kids so she can see how good you are at entertaining rambunctious little ones.

Home Run: Talk about your future family and how many kids you want.

A LEAGUE OF THEIR OWN

The guy hasn't even married you yet and you've probably already named your fourteen children. You're scaring him. Ease up a little.

It's important to talk about your parenting philosophies before you marry, but you'll scare him off if that's your opening conversation on your first date. Guys who weren't raised with younger siblings won't be as natural with children as others who helped raise their younger brothers and sisters, so be patient while they develop skills. Most LDS guys want a family, but they resent being pushed into it before they feel they're ready.

Chapter 22

BATTING PRACTICE

DEFINING THE RELATIONSHIP: SAYING "I LOVE YOU"

It's that L-word that seems to throw everyone into a loop. Whoever says "I love you" first can have an impact on how the rest of the relationship will go. If you say it first and she's not that into you, you've become Cooper's definition of an AFC (average frustrated chump). If she says it first and you're not feeling it, then you've potentially got a girl who can make your time together pretty awkward.

Confessing your love is a leap of faith. You say it hoping she's going to return those magical words. It establishes a contract of sorts, one that requires you to date exclusively. So if you're still picking your batting lineup of girls, don't toss around those three words. Girls take those words seriously. If you say them too early, you may make the whole relationship feel trivial or make her feel like things are moving more quickly than she's comfortable with. Some people will tell guys to never be the one to say "I love you" first. I disagree, but making the relationship too serious too fast can be a problem. A general rule of thumb is to wait at least five dates or sixty days.

Before you profess your undying devotion with those three important words, make sure what you feel really is love. Determine the differences between love, infatuation, and lust, and make sure it's genuine love you feel for her. Here are some guidelines:

Lust:

- You want to make out with her constantly.
- You're dating her because your friends will be jealous.
- You spend more time kissing than talking.
- You can picture her in a bathing suit but not a pioneer costume.
- You don't really have many things in common.
- You think more about her body than her inner qualities.
- You mostly cuddle and look for opportunities to be alone than participate in activities that involve other people or standing apart from each other.
- Your eyes wander to other girls.

Infatuation:

- You can't stop talking about her.
- You see no flaws or weaknesses in her.
- You get sweaty palms and you're a little bit nervous around her.
- You're always on your best behavior.
- You can't wait to learn more about her.
- She seems mysterious to you.
- You think about her all day long.

Love:

- You care more about her needs than yours.
- You want to serve her and make her happy.
- You can picture yourself spending the rest of your life with her.
- You would still want to marry her if she were in a disfiguring car accident.
- You can't imagine your life without her.
- She makes you want to be a better man.
- You think she would be a great mother to your children.
- You're proud of her.
- Your life is better because of her.
- It grows stronger every day.

If you decide to be the first one to confess your love, don't expect a response immediately. You may have surprised her, so give her a few minutes to process what you've just said. If she is silent or says that she doesn't feel the same way, don't apologize for the way you feel. If she jumps to the punch line first and you don't feel the same after analyzing your own feelings, then you'll need to let her know how you feel. Don't drag it on to avoid hurting her. Ending a relationship is never easy. You may still be fond of her, but don't lead her on. Make it clear that the relationship is ending and don't leave her with lingering hope if you know she's not the right one.

COACH COOPER

Defining the relationship (DTR) means having a conversation where you and your special someone try to decide exactly what you are. The sexual tension that's created when neither is quite sure how the other feels is important in building initial attraction. When you're flirting with someone or you're on a date, she knows you're interested. Your male logical mind wants to be open and honest, and you want to know if she's attracted to you so that you can start a real relationship. The female mind wants clarity too. After several dates, she's probably wondering if you two are a couple and trying to decide how to talk about you to her friends. If things are going well, then that DTR will probably occur soon. She may be ready to have that discussion before you are.

It's okay to be vulnerable, and it's also okay if you don't know what you want yet. Women want you to be open and honest. If you're not ready to commit to an exclusive relationship yet, then just assure her that you love her company and want more time to get to know her because you take relationships seriously. That kindly lets her know that your depth of commitment will be worth waiting for and to not rush things.

STATS

- In one study, couples who were asked to recall a moment that involved shared laughter reported being more satisfied in their relationship than those prompted to recall positive moments in their relationship.[131]
- Think positive. Couples who can put a positive spin on their marriage have a 94 percent chance of experiencing a happy future together.[132]
- When the weather turns cold, so do many relationships. It's called the "relationship freeze" when many couples break up or decide to around the holidays. Divorce attorneys see an uptick in business in January, immediately following the holiday season.[133]

- Signs that a man is about to break up with a woman include: he spends less time with her, he is no longer romantic, his passionate kissing turns into quick pecks, he pats her during a hug, and he tries to start fights.[134]

ASSIGNMENTS

First Base: Define to yourself how you truly feel about her. Is it lust, infatuation, or love?

Second Base: Evaluate if you or she wants to date other people still.

Third Base: Write a list of all the reasons why you think you love her. You can even share that list with her if you think she feels the same way.

Home Run: Confess your love to her a creative, romantic way.

A LEAGUE OF THEIR OWN

Some girls are pretty quick to fall in love. We love the idea of being in love, we watch chick flicks about true love, and we've been fantasizing about what the perfect man is like ever since we were little girls. Blurting out "I love you" too soon could scare a guy off. He's trying to get to know you, so don't expect the fairy-tale love-at-first-sight experience.

Enjoy your dates, but don't begin picking out the wedding dress just yet. Mormon girls have the reputation of falling in love hard and fast, so take it easy. Don't scare him off.

You've probably heard about the anxious returned missionary who proposes on the first date, explaining that he was told by the Lord in the temple to marry you. Be careful. You need to have your own personal witness from the Lord. Counsel with the Lord as you choose your eternal companion. He knows who is best for you, and He'll help you identify the right man as you talk and listen in sincere prayer.

Chapter 23

CLOCK *on the* SCOREBOARD

MID-SINGLE ADULTS

Being single in the Church is difficult. Your experience as an older single adult, especially if you have children, is different from what the young guys go through. My sister became a widow a few years ago and was thrust into the dating world when she thought it was forever behind her. She shared with me some interesting insights that I knew had to be included in this book.

Belonging to a Church that focuses on families is further complicated when older LDS singles take a previous temple sealing into account. When my sister began dating again after the death of her young husband, she was shocked to learn that the first question the older LDS single men asked her was, "Have you been sealed?" When she replied yes, they didn't want anything to do with her. She understood why they reacted the way they did, but it was still extremely frustrating. That clock on the scoreboard is ticking away.

Another thing she has learned is that the majority of older men in the LDS single market are hurting. If they are widowers, they are in pain because of the loss they feel from the death of their loved one. If they have been divorced, they are in pain because of the marriage that failed and the loneliness that followed. Each has his share of deep personal wounds. She felt many of the men in the mid-singles scene were not yet in an emotionally healthy state to be dating and they needed to heal first. Instead of reaching out for a new woman to fill the void, recovering single men first need to reach out to the Savior to heal their hearts through the Atonement. I thought that insight was profound. Just because you want to be with someone doesn't mean you're actually ready.

Some older single adults relax their Church standards, rationalizing that they have been valiant and worthy but haven't received the blessings they desire. Loneliness, depression, and the perceived lack of blessings can tempt you to turn away from the Lord's commandments and to stop honoring your personal covenants. That's why enduring to the end is so important. Continued obedience can provide spiritual and emotional protection. There are special challenges when trying to date as an older single adult in the Church, but you'll begin a new relationship in a stronger, healthier position when you maintain your standards and your testimony.

AARP did a study that revealed challenges unique to dating older single women (40+):

- Many have set habits and routines and are less likely to change.
- Divorce and failed relationships add emotional baggage.
- Children and elderly parents can complicate dating with demands and priorities.
- Wrinkles, extra pounds, and other physical-appearance changes diminish self-esteem and create intimacy issues.
- Older women are often more interested in companionship than sex.

- Many are independent and enjoy their freedom, so they're not eager to return to caring for a man's needs like a young bride might be.[137]

A big mistake some divorced men make when dating new women is blaming their ex for everything. When you point out all of the things your ex did wrong, that tells the new girl you haven't fully accepted your role in the divorce. Believe it or not, there were things you did that contributed to your divorce.

If you have children from a prior marriage, move slowly when introducing your new girlfriend to the children. It can be confusing for young children and can feel like a hostile betrayal to older children. You are no longer a single guy dating a single woman; you are merging families together in a complicated way, so be extra sensitive about everyone's feelings and the group dynamics.

If you have children under eighteen years of age, your main priority should be raising them, not dating like crazy. They will only be in your home for a few short years, and then you'll have the rest of your life to date all you want.

Studies show that second marriages have a higher failure rate than first marriages. That's partly because there is more emotional baggage than before. If you haven't learned from your mistakes the first time around, you're more likely to repeat them. Now, that's not to say that they can't work. My parents divorced when I was ten years old, and they have since then remarried and experienced happiness in their second marriages for over forty years.

COACH COOPER

SEEDING A DATE

While talking to a girl you want to ask out, instead of just inviting her on a date, you can build more excitement by seeding the date. Try mentioning the date location during the conversation without actually inviting her. For example, if there is a really cool restaurant you like, say, "I found this great pizza place that has an African theme. Pizza and Africa don't really have anything in common, but they have a big African tree inside, and every time you buy a pizza, they donate a meal to a child." By talking about a neat place or event, you're planting a seed of interest. As you change the subject to something else, she'll remember it and might even be surprised, thinking that you were going to ask her to go there. Later on, almost as an afterthought, you can ask her out. "Hey, remember that pizza place I mentioned earlier? I really want to go again. Are you free tomorrow night? You should come with me."

I've noticed that by seeding a date, the woman will sometimes ask you out or at least hint that she would like to go with you. I was talking with a girl and mentioned a Church activity I was going to the next day. Later in the conversation, she brought it up again, said she really wanted to go, and asked if I would pick her up so we could go together. Try seeding a date, and you'll notice that asking the girl out feels much more natural. She might even beat you to it.

STATS

- According to the Pew Internet and American Life Project, 74 percent of the 10 million Internet users have pursued their romantic interests online.[138]
- The average online romance seeker belongs to three sites and spends an average of $239 per year for online subscriptions.[139]

- A study published in the *Biology of Reproduction* in 2009 showed that male mice who lived with females remained fertile longer than male mice living solo.[140]
- Happy couples talk more. People in the most successful marriages spend more than five hours a week being together and having meaningful conversations. Don't just talk about your calendar and daily chores. Try to really connect on a deeper level.[141]
- Couples who have new experiences together report feeling more loving and supportive toward one another and more satisfied with their marriages.[142]
- Couples in the happiest relationships bring out the best in each other. They help each other get closer to becoming their ideal selves.[143]

ASSIGNMENTS

First Base: Ask yourself why you want to begin dating again.

Second Base: Ask yourself what you learned from your first marriage or from a previous relationship. What did you do wrong? What did you do right?

Third Base: Make a list of your expectations for a future marriage. What compromises are you willing to make?

Home Run: Take an honest look at yourself. Ask yourself the hard questions. (See the list below in "A League of Their Own.") Learn how to tell if you are healed from your pain. Learn to feel love and forgiveness for your ex-wife. Think about what you can give to a new relationship rather than receive.

A LEAGUE OF THEIR OWN

Recently, there have been an alarming number of divorces among couples in my ward everyone thought were strong and unbreakable. In every case, the men left beautiful wives for another woman. When I say "beautiful," I mean truly gorgeous women that everyone thinks are pretty inside and out.

I don't claim to know what goes on behind closed doors, but from a distance, it seems that the men are allowing their eyes to wander and explore other green pastures. It's easy for women to say they're just dogs and scoundrels, but a good man generally doesn't leave a wife who is meeting his needs. If you're divorced and back in the singles scene, be honest with yourself and ask some of the hard questions:

- Did I make him feel like my hero, or did I constantly point out his faults?
- Did he get enough sex, or did I withhold it and use it as a weapon?
- Did I raise him up or belittle him?
- Did I let him lead, or did I insist on being the boss in the relationship?
- Did I nag and nitpick over little things, or was I flexible and able to compromise?
- Did I argue about everything, or was I fun to be around?
- Did I focus on our children and treat him as secondary in my life?
- Was I high maintenance or easy to please?

Divorces are extremely complicated. It's never one person's fault. If you can take ownership of the role you played in your divorce and commit yourself to making the necessary changes, then you're well on your way to a healthy second marriage.

Chapter 24

WORLD SERIES

THE PROPOSAL

For the purposes of this book and baseball theme, I consider the World Series to be your big proposal and engagement. If you're married and you've already conquered that exciting period of your relationship, then the equivalent of the World Series for you is your anniversary and Valentine's Day. Those are two big days when you can really knock it out of the park. Own it; don't blow it.

First, let's talk about the proposal. This is a big deal to most girls. She will be retelling every minute of this story to everyone and anyone who will listen for the rest of her life, so make it good. You need to put some thought into this one so that it's epic and worthy of a crowd around your girl, listening to the blow-by-blow action as she showcases how awesome you are.

Your girl is simple, you say? No fireworks necessary? Fine, but at least get down on one knee and open the velvet-lined ring box so she can relive that classic moment. Think of a speech; don't expect to rise to the occasion by winging it. You're going to be nervous and, face it, she's probably going to memorize those words coming out of your mouth, so they better be romantic.

The most important aspect of the proposal is to do something that is meaningful and unique to you two as a couple. For example, my niece writes comics, so her husband created a little comic book for her to read on their special date. At the end, he drew himself proposing to her and attached a pen where she could answer his question in a blank comment bubble. She loved it.

Here are a few proposal ideas to get your creative juices flowing:

- Take her on a scavenger hunt that recreates locations where you have shared significant memories.
- Put the ring box in the bottom of a box filled with rose petals and two live butterflies. When she opens the box, the butterflies will fly out and she'll be in awe.
- Take her to a Hawaiian restaurant and attach the wedding ring to a lei that you present to her. You could also visit the restaurant ahead of time and ask the waiter to deliver it to your table during a designated moment.
- Buy a sand dollar and write "I love you" on the back of it. Take her for a walk on the beach and suddenly "find" it in the sand. While she's reading the back of the sand dollar, get down on one knee and work your magic.
- Create a photo of the two of you decked out in wedding gear with the phrase "Will you marry me?" on the bottom.
- Write "Will you marry me?" in glow-in-the-dark letters or stars on your ceiling. Turn off the lights and get down on one knee as she reads your message.
- Buy a ball of string and tie the beginning of the string on the front doorknob of your house or apartment. Put a sign at the front door telling her to follow the string and that at the end, there will be a surprise. Trail the string all around your home,

threading it through things and over and under furniture. At the end, you will be waiting with the string tied to the ring.

- Give her a balloon bouquet filled with rose petals. You can take the rose petals with you to the balloon shop and have them placed inside as they fill the balloons with helium. Have the ring placed inside one of the balloons with rose petals. Surprise her with the balloons, and as you pop them, she'll be showered with rose petals and an engagement ring.
- If she is a theater buff, ask the stage manager if you can propose on the stage after the cast's curtain call.
- Arrange a proposal with a street caricaturist. Have him sketch a picture of you two with word bubbles. Yours will read, "Will you marry me?" And hers will say, "Yes!"
- If you two love going to the movies together, the theater will sell you an ad spot where you can design a visual proposal that will run before the trailers begin.
- Make a high tech scavenger hunt. Send her a text message leading her to a secret spot. Keep her engaged by texting her sweet nothings along the way (and directions, of course) as you lead her to you, on bended knee.
- Create a personalized fortune cookie with your own proposal message. You can easily find recipes online to bake them yourself or purchase some that will enable you to switch out messages.
- Make your own message in a bottle. Hide a bottle at the beach with your love note inside. You can dig a sandcastle and "accidentally" find it.
- Reenact her favorite romantic movie. For example, if she loves *Pretty Woman*, you could rent a white limo and climb through the moon roof with flowers in hand to proclaim your love as you arrive at her place.

- Freeze the ring inside an ice cube. Give her a favorite drink with ice and surprise her when she finds a ring inside the ice cube.
- Ask the waiter at an expensive restaurant to place the ring on a dessert tray that he will present to her at the end of the meal.
- If you live near a carnival, boardwalk, or amusement park, win a game for her. When you do, have the game operator hand her the prize: a diamond ring!
- Carefully open a box of Cracker Jacks, steam open the prize packet, place the engagement ring in, and then glue packet and box closed again. Casually give her the box of Cracker Jacks during a movie and watch closely as she opens the prize.
- Propose where you first met. It's a classic.

By the way, think twice before you propose in front of the family. It's risky and your performance will be judged by every woman in the room. Another item to remember is to ask for your bride-to-be's hand in marriage *before* you propose. Do it right and contact her father. I know there are situations where that won't work, but if he's alive and in her life, make the effort.

A quick caution about the engagement: stay committed to keeping the law of chastity. You may be tempted to "enjoy marital benefits," rationalizing that you're going to be married soon anyway. Schedule a short engagement so that you have enough time to plan your wedding, but not so long that you get in trouble. Partaking of honeymoon activities before the actual honeymoon can ruin everything. You've worked hard to find the right girl and be the right guy; don't destroy what you've built with a moment of weakness.

Once she has said yes, enjoy this exciting stage of your life. Volumes have been written about wedding planning, so there is no way I can fit in all of my advice within these pages. Let me just say that your fiancée may get a little crazy about all of the planning. Some girls have been fantasizing about it for years, so she may have specific opinions on how everything should be. Weddings tend to spotlight the bride, so let her have her moment. The flavor of the cake is certainly not worth fighting over. Focus on the merging of your two families and celebrate the romance and love of the occasion.

COACH COOPER

I don't have a long list of proposal ideas for you, but here's something to think about: Have you heard of or do you know someone who proposed and got told no? You should be talking about marriage long before actually proposing. Ideally, you're both openly talking about marriage and you've decided together that you want to get married. She knows you're going to propose, but just doesn't know when you're actually going to propose.

As was stated above, she'll be telling the story of how you proposed for the rest of your lives, so go all out and make it a big deal. She will most likely hint at what kind of proposal she would like. For example, some girls absolutely do not want to be proposed to at a sports game. Other girls dream of being proposed to in front of the castle at Disneyland. If they have strong opinions like that, they'll let you know.

When it comes to picking out a ring, some girls know exactly what they want and others would rather you pick something out. Most couples go ring shopping together before getting engaged, but if you really want to make it a surprise, you'll have to do some stealth work. In addition to picking a ring out, you'll have to find out her ring size. You'll have to involve one of her friends or roommates, if that's what you're going for. Her friend can find out her ring size or snag one of her rings (that she wears on the correct ring finger) that you can take to a jewelry store to find out what size she wears.

STATS

- Men are put off by groups of loud women. If a woman wants to get a date, she should break away from a loud group to give a man a chance to approach her.
- If you want to create an instant link with a date, say his or her name at least two times in the conversation to show connectedness.
- Women have a stronger sense of smell than men and are particularly attracted to musk colognes and pheromone-based aftershaves.[146]
- When a man first approaches a woman, she will base 55 percent of her initial impression of him on his appearance and body language, 38 percent on his style of speaking, and 7 percent on what he actually says.[147]

ASSIGNMENTS

First Base: Pray to Heavenly Father first to find out if you really should marry this girl. Really listen. This decision will affect the quality of the rest of your life.

Second Base: Ask her father for her hand in marriage.

Third Base: Create a truly memorable proposal. Wherever you do it, kneel down on one knee, present a beautiful ring, and tell her she would make you the luckiest man in the world if she would be your wife.

Home Run: Have someone film you proposing to your wife so you can share that monumental memory with your posterity.

A LEAGUE OF THEIR OWN

As your relationship gets more serious, be sure to get a strong confirmation from the Lord that this is the right guy for you. Once married, there will be days when you both drive each other crazy and you wonder if you made a mistake, so be sure you have a strong answer from Heavenly Father.

If he proposes before you're sure he's the right man for you, don't feel pressured to give him an answer on the spot. There's nothing wrong with saying, "I love you, but I need time to give you my answer." Yeah, that's not exactly the most romantic proposal scenario you've pictured in your mind, but it's better to be sure than divorced later on.

FOR MARRIED GUYS

Chapter 25

NEGOTIATING *the* CONTRACT

YOUR ONE AND ONLY

You've signed the contract, and now you're finally married. Congratulations! Being married is awesome. You get to spend the rest of your life with your best friend at your side, cheering you on, loving you, helping you, inspiring you, and making every day an exciting adventure. Marriage was made in heaven, but the maintenance has to be done here on earth. You're now a team, and together you can conquer the world, loving and *serving* each other one day at a time.

The honeymoon phase of marriage is so much fun as you discover each other in new ways and learn to create a life together. There is definitely an adjustment period as you transition from being a carefree, single guy to a responsible married man. Keep a sense of humor about all of the changes and remember that this is all new for her too. There needs to be a lot of compromise from both of you during the negotiation process as you merge two families together and select which traditions, ideologies, and values you will incorporate into your new family.

I asked my husband what profound marriage advice he had that I could share with you. His advice for husbands and wives was to not go into marriage thinking it's a 50/50 proposition. You both have to give 100 percent, and sometimes more. There will be days when one of you will have to give more to make up for any slack. It's all a give and take. In marriages that struggle, each partner thinks he or she is giving more than the other and becomes resentful. We often overvalue our own efforts, not realizing how much the other person might be sacrificing or giving to make the marriage work. Perception is not the same thing as reality.

Marriage is a constantly evolving experience. You will need to adapt your patterns and habits every time a baby is added to your family, there is a new job, or you move to a new city. Take control of those big moments in life and sit down together to come up with a working plan that will strengthen and enrich your marriage. Don't let changing circumstances cause you to lose sight of each other. You're in this together now. It's going to be great!

One of the big changes now is in your relationship status. It's the day that your new bride has been dreaming of. You've probably been flirting for many years, but now it's time to take yourself off the market. One wrong, playful look at another woman, and you'll be on the bench. Put on your blinders and stay focused on your wife. President Thomas S. Monson wisely counseled married couples to "Choose your love and love your choice."[148]

Hanging out with old girlfriends, going out to lunch alone with a female coworker, or chatting online with other women is simply inappropriate now. You may think your intentions are innocent, but that's how affairs begin. Guard your marriage vigilantly. If you wouldn't behave a certain way in front of your wife, then you know you're crossing the line.

So, what do you do when another woman pursues you? Be a man. Be a married man. Sure, it's flattering, but don't provide the smallest opening for flirtation. Always wear your wedding ring. If the tempting little vixen is not getting the hint, talk about how great your wife is. It's better to be rude to her than to head to divorce court or a Church disciplinary hearing because of your infidelity. And by the way, you don't necessarily have to have sex to be unfaithful to your wife.

What if a woman does hit on you at work? Should you tell your wife? What will she think? What are the consequences of telling or not telling your wife? Here are some pros and cons of telling her when someone is being flirtatious with you.

Pros:

- You're honest with your wife and there are no secrets between you. There is great peace in honesty.
- It gives you an opportunity to remind your wife how much you love her and only her.
- She might be able to give you tips on how to get rid of the unwanted attention.

Cons:

- You might be inflicting unnecessary pain and worry on your wife.
- She may begin to mistrust you, constantly wondering if you're subconsciously welcoming flirtations from other women.
- You might be creating a distance between you and your wife, causing her to feel her marriage isn't safe.

STATS

- One out of three teens has had a violent experience in a relationship.[149]

- 51 percent of single people surveyed say that flattery is the best way to attract someone.[150]
- The number one relationship argument is over money.
- 63 percent of married couples claim to have found their mates through a network of friends.[151]

ASSIGNMENTS

First Base: Always wear your wedding ring.

Second Base: Put pictures of your wife on your desk at work.

Third Base: Invite your wife out for lunch so your female coworkers or classmates can see you happily spending time with her.

Home Run: Invite your wife to office parties or other events where other women can see you together and know you are happily married and off the market. Introduce her as your "one and only" or "true love." Other women will usually swoon and want your marriage to succeed.

A LEAGUE OF THEIR OWN

Girls, you're now dressing to impress your husband, not all those other guys out there who might still be checking you out. Be modest and tasteful both before and after marriage. Make it clear to other men that you are now married and off the market. Put your blinders on. Don't spend a minute thinking about what it would be like to be married to someone else, and be careful not to compare your husband with your friends' husbands.

You married your husband because you love him, so don't start focusing on all his imperfections. You have plenty of them too. He's learning how to negotiate a new life with a woman who thinks differently than he does. He's new at being a husband, just like you're new at being a wife. Have patience with each other as you learn how to be better spouses.

A good friend in my ward shared this with me about her recent divorce:

> I can tell you that teams are successful because they play together with a common goal. I think couples forget to set that goal. I often think women want guys to be like Babe Ruth, when in fact, they are just at the tee ball stage. We would never expect our five-year-old son to do anything more in the outfield than stand on his glove and catch butterflies. However, we expect men to hit these home runs all the time. I think marriage takes a lot of willingness to allow the other person to learn to be better and a ton of forgiveness. Like in baseball, there will be moments of greatness, boredom, laughter, great defeat, and applause.

Chapter 26

CURVE BALL

DOES THIS MAKE ME LOOK FAT?

When **pitchers throw a** curve ball, they put a twist on it at the last moment that causes the ball to spin diagonally or from side to side, rather than a straight backspin like a fastball. That last-second spin causes the air around the ball to travel faster at the bottom of the ball's surface than it does at the top. Because it's going faster on the bottom, the ball will suddenly veer downward just before it gets to the batter. A batter only has about one-fifth of a second to realize what's happening, so it makes it extremely difficult for him to make contact.

What's the male-female relationship equivalent to the curve ball? It's when you're not sure how to answer a question or behave because you're afraid you're going to blow it. The classic example is when a woman asks, "Does this make me look fat?" You have a split second to come up with an acceptable answer, and you know that pretty much no matter what you say, it's not going to be the right thing. Sorry guys. We really don't mean to put you in such a difficult position intentionally.

Every married man knows that there are simply certain days in the month when all a man has to do is open his mouth and he takes his life into his own hands. Women don't want to be hostages to their fluctuating hormones, but that monthly cycle can sometimes have an extremely strong power over their emotions and brains. Be warned: telling her that she's irrational because it's her time of the month *could* help, but it might only make matters worse.

Here are some tips on how to survive those dangerous moments: what to say and what *not* to say.

FOOD CONVERSATION

Dangerous: What's for dinner?
Default: Have some chocolate.
Safer: Can I help you with dinner?
Safest: Where would you like to go for dinner?

CLOTHING CHOICES

Dangerous: Are you wearing that?
Default: Have some chocolate.
Safer: You know what outfit I especially love on you? I'd love to see you wear____.
Safest: Wow! Look at you!

EMOTIONS

Dangerous: What are you so worked up about?
Default: Have some chocolate.
Safer: Are you feeling okay?
Safest: I'm listening.

DIETING

Dangerous: Should you be eating that?
Default: Have some chocolate.
Safer: There are a lot of apples left.
Safest: (Silence)

HOUSEWORK

Dangerous: What did you do all day?
Default: Have some chocolate.
Safer: I hope you didn't overdo it today.
Safest: I've always loved you in that robe!

Of course, the examples above are meant to make you laugh, but the concept is still true. There is always a gentler way to say something to a woman. What's the deal with chocolate anyway?

STATS

- Discovery.com offers a scientific explanation for why men have a hard time listening to women. They say that since women's voices have many more frequencies than men's, the male brain must work harder to analyze sound frequencies and comprehend the meaning intended.[154]
- Typically, men's brains are 11–12 percent bigger than women's brains. This difference in size has absolutely nothing to do with intelligence.[155]
- Psychologist Shelly E. Taylor said, "In stress situations, men have a response reaction that resembles 'fight or flight' while women tend to react with a 'tend and befriend' strategy.[156]

ASSIGNMENTS

First Base: If you're unsure, ask her, "Is this a test? Is this a trick question? Is it possible for me to come out smelling like a rose after this request, or will I just smell bad?" If you use humor, she may back off and give you an A on the test anyway.

Second Base: Prepare a list of possible humorous answers to questions you think she'll ask you, such as, "Does this make me look fat?" When she asks, you can even jokingly answer, "Let me get my list of acceptable answers so that I don't blow it."

Third Base: Put your arms around her waist and tell her how much you love her. Maybe that will distract her long enough that you won't need to answer the question.

Home Run: Buy your wife a new outfit.

"Life is like a baseball game. When you think a fastball is coming, you gotta be ready to hit the curve."
—Jaja Q.[152]

A LEAGUE OF THEIR OWN

Don't ask a man a question you really don't want an honest answer to. He's going to feel trapped, confused, and frustrated. Ask your girlfriends how you look in certain outfits; they'll be honest with you and won't be concerned about whether or not your relationship is over when you hear the truth.

Don't be a high-maintenance wife who asks her man to do things you can easily do for yourself. If you're craving pumpkin ice cream when you're pregnant, go out and buy it yourself. If he asks if there is anything he can do for you, *then* you can ask him to run to the store. Afterward, let him know he is your hero so that he's rewarded for his efforts. There are other ways you can reward him as well. When he feels like his efforts are appreciated and rewarded, he'll go to the ends of the earth for you.

Chapter 27

SCORE!

HOW DO I GET MORE SEX?

If you saw the word *sex* in the table of contents, then this is probably the first chapter you jumped to. Sex is really fun and a big perk of being married. (You single guys are going to love it once you're married.) It is a beautiful expression of love and definitely worth waiting for. In fact, the first question most guys ask after sex is, "When can we do that again?" I'm going to let you in on some secrets few married men understand about women when it comes to this delicate matter.

SEX SECRET ONE

Husbands, you need to know something. Foreplay starts *outside* the bedroom. It can often begin at the kitchen sink when you say you're going to do the dishes tonight. It can occur when you remember to take out the garbage before she has to nag you to do it. And nothing is more sexy to an exhausted new mother than watching her thoughtful husband change the diapers. I'm not kidding. It's one of the least understood mysteries about women.

It probably seems odd and maybe even unfair to men that housework is connected to sex. An interesting dialogue occurs in her mind that connects the two activities. For example, every time your wife has to pick up your dirty clothes from the floor or put that toilet seat down again, she is thinking to herself, "He must think I'm his personal servant," or, "He knows that bothers me and he does it anyway." I know, to you they're just innocent socks or a meaningless toilet, but to her they are expressions of your love or lack of thoughtfulness. She doesn't want to give herself to someone who doesn't appreciate her. When you are considerate of her time, she'll want to give you more of hers, inside and outside of the bedroom. Give a little more in the kitchen; get a little more in the bedroom.

It really boils down to expectations. They are often determined by what you saw your parents do or even what you saw in the movies or on TV while growing up. For example, did your mom do all the housework? Is that what you expect to happen in your home? Who filled the gas tank? Who took out the garbage? Who goes grocery shopping? Are there certain chores that you consider to be the man's job? The family proclamation does *not* say that housekeeping is a woman's divine purpose.

If you "help" your wife with housework, then that implies that it's her job. If she stays at home to raise your children, then she has a full-time job, just like you. Whose dishes are in the sink? Hers? Nope, they're "ours." If you decide that neither one of you is going to clean the house, that's fine. But you'd have to include housekeeping in your budget so you could afford to pay someone else to do it.

SEX SECRET TWO

Don't expect your wife to be a wild sex kitten in the bedroom on your honeymoon after she has spent her entire lifetime trying to be chaste, clean, and pure. Men have a lot of scenarios running in their head about sex long before they're married, whereas young

brides mostly imagine the loving closeness and romance of it all. Women tend to think more romantically: candles, soft music, a warm embrace, loving words. Men tend to think more sexually: skip all the nonsense and get to the good part. Women want to feel loved before having sex. Men want sex to feel loved. Women want the loving experience; men need the physical release. Are you seeing the difference here?

New brides are often shocked to learn how important sex is to their husband. They imagined endless nights of cuddling and pillow talk with their new husband, not an insatiable desire for wild romps every night and another one in the morning. We get it: you kept yourself morally clean before getting married and, like living in a drought, you now want to turn on the fire hose and enjoy the benefits of being married. Pace yourself. Make sure you're including that cuddling and pillow talk with your sweet bride.

SEX SECRET THREE

Men are visual. They want to see a naked woman. Men are created to be attracted to the female form. Women generally would prefer to "do it" in the dark. They usually think men's tight-fitting bathing suits are disgusting. Their brains just work differently.

A gifting "fly ball" that can go wrong is lingerie. A sexy negligee or nightie is fun to receive as a gift every now and then, but if those are the only kinds of clothing she ever receives from you, she's going to get annoyed. I mean how many of those foreplay outfits does she really need? She'll be more thrilled with a new outfit she can actually wear out in public and brag to her friends that you gave her. She can't show off all those bedroom ensembles to her friends. She wants to be able to talk to her girlfriends about how thoughtful you are. It seems pointless to her to get another sexy little outfit that she's only going to wear for four seconds.

SEX SECRET FOUR

Not many people will talk honestly about this, but men generally enjoy sex more than women. It's a sad, frustrating fact. Anatomically speaking, men are designed to "have fun" every time. For women, it takes a lot more physical and mental work. Physically, it can even be painful for women at times, something that rarely happens with men. Emotionally speaking, women have to think about getting pregnant before and after. A woman's entire life can be altered with only one encounter, and she knows it. That rarely occurs to a man when he's in the mood. A married woman has to consider birth control measures every single day, a fact that could even make her resent sex.

Now guys, there will be times when your wife would rather just go to sleep after a long day than stay awake another hour "playing." She might prefer the encounter to be short, and so she may offer it to you as a loving gift. Accept the gift and don't be offended if that's all that happens. Her lack of passion doesn't mean she doesn't love you. Women want sex to be a special occasion, but if you demand it all the time, it can become a task that she dreads.

SEX SECRET FIVE

She will be more in the mood when she knows she can turn you on. So what if she's had so many pregnancies that her girlish figure looks more like a ghoulish figure? Surely there is *something* good you can say about her body. You need to think of something quick and it had better be sincere. If you're really having a hard time coming up with anything positive to say about her body, then just look in the mirror. You just might not be perfect either.

Let me stop here for one moment to make it perfectly clear that you balance your adoration of her physical qualities with her inner beauty. Women complain that all men want is one thing and that their evaluation of a woman is based entirely on physical attributes. Be careful in your praise of her external gifts to include some of her inner qualities so she knows it is the whole person you love.

You know when you watch some commercial on TV with a catchy jingle and then you can't get that song out of your head all day? If the power of suggestion can affect us that much from a source we really don't care about, think about how much it would affect us if it came from a source we really did care about. When your sweetheart hears you complain about what a terrible cook she is or how you wish her hair looked different, then she begins to believe it. The opposite is true too. When she hears what a thoughtful friend or caring mother she is, then she becomes those. She wants to believe that you will keep pursuing her even after you've won her. She wants to feel like she's worth it to you.

NEW FATHERS

Don't be grabby and needy after the baby is born. Her body is healing, her hormones are going crazy, she's absolutely exhausted, and she probably has had a baby attached to her the majority of the day. Sex is the last thing on her mind. Don't take it personally. She is completely focused on recovering from her pregnancy and delivery, as well as this new little one who needs her completely. Don't be another baby she has to tend to. You should be her refuge, not another chore. Don't worry; this transition period won't last forever, maybe a few months. Man up. She has made many sacrifices for nine months. Make this little one for her.

ASSIGNMENTS FOR NEW DADS

First Base: Tell your baby's new mom she's beautiful. She definitely won't feel beautiful for a while, but she'll melt when she hears you say that she is.

Second Base: Take care of the baby so she can sleep.

Third Base: Take care of the dishes, laundry, housekeeping, and baby so that she can sleep.

Home Run: Present her with a gift to thank her for the amazing gift she has given you of having a baby. Then let her sleep. Do you see a pattern here? She needs to get some sleep.

ASSIGNMENTS FOR ALL MARRIED MEN

First Base: Massage her feet or back.

Second Base: Do the dishes or laundry.

Third Base: Plan a romantic evening where you shower her with declarations of love.

Home Run: Do all of those things listed above, but don't expect sex as your reward. When a woman knows you're being nice because all she thinks you want is sex, it makes her resentful. Let her make love to you as a gift, and you will both enjoy it more.

STATS

- Ten percent of sex offenders use online dating sites to meet people.[159]
- The average length of courtship for marriages that met online is 18.5 months.[160]
- The average length of courtship for marriages that met offline is 42 months.[161]
- The percent of people who believe in love at first sight is 71 percent.[162]

A LEAGUE OF THEIR OWN

Married men need sex to be physically healthy and emotionally happy. Learn to communicate with him what it is you need to be physically healthy and emotionally happy too. Be specific. He won't know unless you tell him. Don't use sex as a weapon to punish your man. Your bedroom should be your sanctuary, not a battle ground.

Wives are often frustrated that their husbands don't help more around the house, yet they won't relinquish control over the housework. Divide up the chores with your husband and then stop caring so much about every little detail. Accept the fact that he won't wipe the counters as perfectly as you think they should be done. His version of a clean toilet may not be yours. Most of those things simply don't matter. When it comes to housekeeping, "good enough" can save your marriage. As soon as I embraced imperfection and felt gratitude for what my husband was doing, life became so much less stressful, and I became a happier wife. In the end, the Lord is going to ask you what you did for your husband to make a good marriage, not how clean your house was. Now go put on your nightie and have fun with your husband.

Chapter 28

SAFE!

COURTSHIP CONTINUES IN MARRIAGE

You may think after the famous words, "You may now kiss the bride," that your mission has been accomplished. But once you are married, the love affair really begins. Continue to have the attitude of courting her, and she will continue to act like a flirtatious young girl. Go on a date night once a week. Date nights are sacred. By the way, you don't necessarily have to spend money or even get out of the house to have a date night.

I know having date nights is easier said than done, but it will strengthen your marriage and be a smart investment for all time and eternity. Make her feel that you consider yourself lucky to have caught her and hold on to her tight so she won't get away. Let her catch you looking at her with awe (in a good way!).

Fall in love over and over again. If you stop nurturing a garden, it dies. So will your marriage. Romance is not a spectator sport. Don't let your marriage just naturally evolve or else your bills, kids, and busy life can easily devolve your romantic relationship into a business partnership or even roommate status. Set a personal goal

to take specific actions each week and month to keep the spark between the two of you alive and strong.

In marriage, the ballpark is your home, where you and your sweetheart create a life together. Your home should be a safe zone, a neutral place without any baggage where you're both equal. In marriage, your bedroom should be your sanctuary. Your wife might want it to be frilly and romantic. If that's what it takes to make her feel safe, sexy, and secure with you, let her do it. A ruffle isn't going to kill you.

Some people advocate that there should not be a TV in the bedroom. Others suggest that if you can hold hands and watch a favorite show together as your evening ritual, then that can become a relaxing, bonding time together that builds a strong relationship. Find what works for you.

STATS

- The American Society for Microbiology says that 90 percent of women wash their hands after using a public restroom, whereas only 75 percent of men do. Despite that, researchers at the University of Colorado found that women carried twice the number of bacteria on their hands as men.[165]
- 80 percent of school discipline is done to boys. 80 percent of high school dropouts are boys and 20 percent are girls.[166]
- According to the US Census Bureau, 14 percent of men between the ages of twenty-five and thirty-four still live with their parents. Only 8 percent of women between the ages of twenty-five and thirty-four live with their parents.[167]

ASSIGNMENTS

First Base: Bring her flowers.
Second Base: Plan a date night.
Third Base: Work on a project together.
Home Run: Frame a picture of you two together and hang it somewhere in your home.

A LEAGUE OF THEIR OWN

Now that you're married, you and your husband can take turns planning fun, creative dates; you don't have to wait for your husband to do it all. A healthy marriage is a combined effort, full of give-and-take moments of compromise.

Make it a habit to sit down and calendar your week together. Sundays are perfect for that. Talk about your strengths and how to improve your weaknesses. No, this is *not* a time to shred your man to pieces. It *is* a time to plan date nights and talk about how you will conquer tasks as a team. You should end your session feeling closer and more united.

Chapter 29

BASEBALL TRIVIA

THE DETAILS COUNT

Your sweetheart is a trivia fanatic, just probably not about baseball. Your girl will remember *everything*. She mentally keeps track of almost everything you do and say. She subconsciously remembers how many times you've opened the door for her, how many times you've rubbed her tired feet, how many times you've forgotten her birthday and a million other little facts. Even more frightening to men is that all of those factoids are connected with an emotion. I don't know why. Women are just built that way.

She'll remember what you ordered to eat at that cute little Italian restaurant where she first went on a date with you. She'll remember what you were wearing when you first held her hand or kissed her. You will be wise to remember those things too if you want to touch her sentimental heart. Pay attention to the details. The small things mean more to women than the big ones. Remember, you win a game with those small, consistent base hits, not necessarily with home runs. She will remember all of the good things you do, and for decades she will brag to her friends about how amazing you are.

On the downside, she can also remember every time you were late, even though you apologized afterward. There is some kind of subconscious accounting that goes on in her brain so that when you and she both think you have been forgiven and the issue has been resolved, it really tends to be stored in the dark recesses of an internal filing cabinet in her heart.

Women find it hard to discuss one issue or episode. They pull out the file that contains every infraction of that relationship law and base their case on character history. We women like to think we're thinking clearly and fairly, but all of that paperwork from past issues keeps filing through our memory, and a pattern emerges that we simply can't dismiss.

In other words, start memorizing some facts of your own: her birthday, your anniversary, the first time you met, your first date. They may just mean numbers to you, but to her they are opportunities for you to show her that she's important to you.

My husband and I were married on August 14, so for most of our marriage we have celebrated the 14th every month of the year in some way to show our love for each other. Sometimes it's a gift, sometimes it's some cake, and sometimes it's just simply a verbal reminder that we're still glad we're married to each other. It's a fun way to make a regular old Tuesday (or whatever day) a great reason to celebrate. In the hum drum of everyday life of paying the bills and driving the kids to soccer practice, it's a great chance to celebrate and find joy.

What if it's really hard to remember? Write it down. Put it on a calendar. Just because it's hard for you to remember all those dates and details doesn't get you out of it.

Do you know all of the answers to the trivia questions about your sweetheart in chapter 2? Ask your wife and then take mental note. You can give your wife any flower and score a base hit, or you can lovingly present her with her *favorite* flower and you'll score a triple! Knowing the details about your wife can make a big difference in how your romantic gestures are received.

STATS

- An average woman in the United Kingdom will own 111 handbags in her lifetime.[170]
- Women in ancient Rome wore the sweat of gladiators to improve their beauty and complexion.[171]
- In Russia, there are 9 million more women than men.[172]
- Men burn fat faster than women by a rate of about fifty calories a day.[173]
- Men get hiccups more often than women.[174]

ASSIGNMENTS

First Base: Comment on a small detail about your wife's jewelry or hairstyle.

Second Base: Begin taking notes of small things she says and does that you like. These tidbits can come in handy when you're trying to think of a thoughtful gift or date night.

Third Base: Begin collecting small items from places where you have gone on dates with her, like a matchbook, napkin, or ticket stub so you can present them to her on a special occasion.

Home Run: Try to recreate your first date with her on your anniversary.

A LEAGUE OF THEIR OWN

Don't expect him to remember all of the details that you do. Guys aren't naturally built that way. There's nothing wrong with your writing down important items on a list and helping him memorize them or placing them on his cell phone. Explain why they're meaningful to you and why you need him to know them. A good friend of mine gives her husband a list of gifts she wants to receive from him so that he can be her hero on her birthday or Christmas. I used to think that took all of the surprise out of gift giving, but now I appreciate her wise idea. How else could a husband possibly know what's on his wife's secret wish list?

Don't be so offended if he forgets. He's not trying to hurt you on purpose. He might not see why it's important. Calmly explain to him why it is and offer to do something that's important to him in exchange. When a guy understands how he will benefit from his efforts, he may be much more motivated.

Chapter 30

ERROR

FINDING FORGIVENESS WHEN YOU STRIKE OUT

G**irls don't want to** marry a lying eight-year-old. They want to marry a man. Don't even think about lying, because she will find out. That being said, you don't have to lie to end up on the bench. Sometimes you won't even know why you're in trouble with your wife; you'll just know you did something wrong. Ask what you did. That sounds easy enough, but some women will get even angrier that she has to tell you. Part of why she's mad is that you don't realize that what you did hurt her. She expects you to read her mind. Just explain that you need complete clarity on the issue so that you won't do it again. Of course, she's not perfect either, but I wouldn't recommend throwing that little nugget in her face at these moments or you'll likely be sitting on the bench even longer.

You will have disagreements. No relationship is perfect all of the time. You don't have to like each other always. You just have to be committed. You'll be completely convinced that you're right, and she'll think she is. Who's actually right? Honestly, it doesn't really matter.

Whenever you and your wife have a problem, don't look for who is to blame. Look inward. Ask yourself, "How did I create or contribute to the problem?" Before you wer married, she was probably watching how you resolved conflicts. That told her how marriage and life would be if she decided to spend it with you. You should be watching how she resolves conflicts too. Peaceful resolution is extremely important in marriage.

RETRACTIONS

Here's an idea you might try: provide a list of humorous, written retractions ahead of time to remind your wife that you're not perfect and you know it. A sense of humor can go a long way. Here are some suggestions:

- I'm sorry that I left the left turn signal on for two miles like an old man.
- I'm sorry that when I coughed to cover my fart noise you still knew I was farting.
- I'm sorry you caught me staring at another woman. I honestly thought it was the old lady I home teach and I was going to ask her for an appointment to swing by.
- I'm sorry I can't take my eyes off of you because you're so beautiful. (She'll roll her eyes, but you'll score points with this one every time.)

Some people say that the past is behind you, but that's not entirely true. Each person brings past experiences and baggage into the relationship. Try to understand your past, but don't dwell on it. You are who you are today based on your past.

Don't encourage insecurities in each other. Once you are married and know each other's secrets, you hold the power to destroy someone. You both need to feel safe with each other.

THE BLAME GAME

There is a story about an old man dying in the hospital with his wife, Ethyl, lovingly sitting at his side. She tenderly holds his hand while he begins to say his last words of farewell to her, reflecting on their life together.

"Ethyl," he begins, "the first year of our marriage, we worked really hard, but we still lost half of our farm. You were always by my side, Ethyl." He continued, "The second year of our marriage, we worked even harder and we still lost the other half of the farm, but you were always by my side, Ethyl. We had five businesses. They all went under, but you were always by my side, Ethyl. We had eleven kids and couldn't afford to educate them, but you were always by my side, Ethyl. After all these years, I've decided you're bad luck, Ethyl!"

Here's the deal: this is *your* life. If your relationship is getting boring, whose fault is that? Don't blame her for everything. Decide to have a better marriage and take action. Fill it with experiences that will enrich your mortal life and teach you things that will make you more Christlike and bring joy to yourself and others.

Don't fix the blame. Fix the problem. You have one shot at life and this is it. You'll waste way too much time being unhappy if you point your finger at anyone other than yourself when things go wrong. You always have a choice on how you will react. For example, if you're in a car accident that leaves your vehicle with a big smash in the side door, how will you react?

- Blame the other guy, sue him, and get revenge.
- Get mad and whine and complain for weeks.
- Get depressed and convince yourself that you're stupid.
- Calmly file a police report and call your insurance company.
- After calmly taking care of the situation, be grateful you weren't hurt and say, "Boy, am I blessed!"

STATS

- The feeling of being head-over-heels in love is the result of raised levels of protein in your bloodstream.[177]
- The average wedding costs $20,000.[178]
- The average divorce costs between $15,000 and $20,000.[179]
- 60 percent of divorces occur within the first ten years of marriage.[180]
- Men have six times more testosterone than women. Testosterone is linked to aggression and hostility and impairs the impulse-control region of the brain.[181]

- Studies show that men in stable relationships tend to be healthier, live longer, and have hormone levels that may indicate decreased anxiety.[182]

ASSIGNMENTS

First Base: Say you're sorry. Mean it.

Second Base: Keep a supply of romantic cards somewhere so that you can whip one out and ask forgiveness, even if you're not quite sure what you did.

Third Base: Bring her a bouquet of flowers with a card.

Home Run: Make sure you forgive her and do what it takes for her to forgive you.

A LEAGUE OF THEIR OWN

You're not perfect yet, so stop expecting your husband to be. He probably won't do things exactly the way you think they should be done. You need to be more flexible or you're going to drive him away. Every time you nitpick over some dumb thing, like the way he washes the dishes or leaves the toilet seat up, you're driving a wedge between the two of you. Yes, you can gently remind him, but throwing a tantrum is definitely not going to endear him to you.

Just let the little things go. Is he a man of integrity? That's a big thing. If he is, then who cares how he squeezes the toothpaste tube? Just buy a separate tube for yourself. Is he kind? That's a big thing too. If he is, then don't make a big deal out of the fact that he doesn't wipe the kitchen counter exactly the way you think it should be done. Pick your battles.

Chapter 31

BREAKING *in a* NEW GLOVE

BE PATIENT: WOMEN DON'T KNOW WHAT THEY WANT EITHER

Whenever my husband is on the bench, he brings me flowers. That used to make me even more angry. I considered the money he spent on them a waste. I thought that money could have gone toward something more practical that we needed, like paying the water bill or buying diapers or new shoes for one of the kids. Just to throw me off, he'd bring me flowers when he wasn't on the bench. I have always loved flowers, but I still resisted the loving gesture because I'm terribly cheap at heart and knew we had important bills to pay. Finally, I decided the money spent on those flowers was still cheaper than marriage counseling or a divorce attorney. So, what is my point? I think my husband was trying to break in a new glove; he had to keep working with me until I would soften. He just wants to give me something he thinks will make me happy.

Another example of this is women who don't allow their husbands to be gentlemen and open doors for them. Of course women are completely capable of opening their own doors. Some feminist women are so adamant about proving to the world that they're equally capable as men that they forget to be women. If you find yourself with one of these stubborn women, then just keep opening the door for her anyway. She may resist for a while at first, but deep down, she is glowing inside that she has found such a man. She wants to feel special and important to you. Insist on being a gentleman, and soon that soft woman inside will emerge and she'll feel more comfortable.

My friend, Tristi Pinkston, said, "I wish guys knew that we confuse ourselves too. We don't just confuse them. Sometimes we really don't know what we want. We just know we don't want whatever it is you just did or said or bought."

Have you experienced this frustrating conversation before?

You: What do you want?

Her: I don't know.

You: How about this?

Her: No.

You: How about that?

Her: No.

You: So . . .

One way to overcome a woman's inability to know what she wants sometimes is to find out what she doesn't want. Be patient and offer suggestions. You can seed her thoughts by giving her options to choose from. By a process of elimination, you may both discover the answer.

Whether it's choosing what to order on the menu at a restaurant or what color to paint the walls in the living room, sometimes a woman's inability to decide on something comes from the fear she has about making the wrong choice. Assure her that everything is going to be fine. She needs your calm voice of reason and logic, but she mostly needs your patience.

My husband often gets frustrated when he sees a woman in the car in front of him taking forever to pull out into an intersection.

Maybe it's a girl thing, but we're not trying to drive you guys crazy with our driving habits. Consider that she might be driving a car she's unfamiliar with and she doesn't know how much "get up and go" the car has in order to quickly pass through the intersection without crashing into another car. She might be driving a sick child to the doctor's office and she doesn't want to jolt the car too fast or the kid might throw up. The point is that women operate on a different time table than men do. Just be patient and grateful that you have this lovely lady to spend eternity with, even if it takes her that long to drive through an intersection.

STATS

- 43 percent of singles are likely to have looked up someone online before a first date.[184]
- 29 percent of women would rather spend their efforts shoe shopping than prowling around for men.[185]
- The number one buzz kill on a first date is a conversation about past relationships (49 percent), with dieting or body image coming in at number two.[186]

ASSIGNMENTS

First Base: Write a list of possible choices for her. Help her brainstorm.

Second Base: Talk about the pros and cons of making a certain choice.

Third Base: Assure her you're happy with her decision.

Home Run: Be patient while she decides what she wants.

A LEAGUE OF THEIR OWN

Men generally don't live in the details like women do. Don't expect him to care whether the paint color on the wall is "Almond Bliss" or "Baker's Tan." He mostly just wants you to be happy. Don't stress out over all the little things. Try to appreciate the big things he's doing right and that are going well in your life.

Men are usually quick decision makers. Thank him for being patient with you as you contemplate every possible scenario before making your choice. Laugh at your differences and be considerate.

Chapter 32

TRADING CARDS

WHAT SHE'LL KEEP AND WHAT SHE'LL TOSS

W**omen are sentimental creatures.** They are created with some kind of mysterious gene that compels them to save mementos and scrapbook. They love to see and save beautiful things. It's just the way it is. Yes, there are women who are exceptions to this, but they are rare.

All of the little things she puts in her scrapbooks remind her how wonderful you are. When your wife saves some kind of token that involves you, that's a good sign. She has already pictured showing that item to her grandchildren and telling them all about how you two met. Saving that ticket stub or flower petal means she wants you to be around for a long time.

The larger her stash is of sentimental items, the more proof she has that you're romantic and awesome. So, what's the lesson? You need to provide her with lots of evidence.

Girls love sentimental guys—manly, but sentimental. Any day could be an occasion for a loving card from you. Email cards are fine, but make one by hand or actually go to the store and pick out a real paper card every now and then. What's fun is when you add cute, personal drawings and inside jokes to the card. Yes, you probably ought to buy a card on Valentine's Day. That, plus flowers, is the bare minimum.

When my children were little, my husband left for work in the early hours, long before the rest of us headed to the kitchen table for our breakfast. Every day we would find sweet notes written to us by my husband. He would draw entertaining pictures for our sons and write loving words of appreciation to me. Those base hits added up quickly to create a home run effect. I still have every one of those notes.

A silly tradition that was spontaneously started many years ago in our marriage was hiding a particular card over and over for each other to find. For example, I would hide it under my husband's

pillow. He would find it and then hide it in my sock drawer. I would find it and then hide it in the glove compartment of his car. And so the game would continue. Sometimes it would take longer to find it than other times, but the discovery always led to a smile and a laugh. On the card were written the words "I love you," so each time it reappeared, the finder would feel loved all over again.

Texting cute, flirty messages to your honey during the day will help her feel loved and might provide a happy night after you get home.

Do you have a hoarder on your hands? It's hard for women to let go of mementos, so if your house is overflowing with items from years gone by, help her release her grasp gently. Don't just throw them out or you'll have war and tears. Women are imagining every possible scenario where they might need that item again in the future. Offer to scan documents or take pictures of items to free up some space. Mention the tax benefits you'll receive by donating the items. Some couples establish a rule that before a new thing comes into the house, an old one has to leave. A woman wants to feel safe and secure, so assure her that your love will always remain even after she tosses those 482 plastic cups that are stuffed into your kitchen cabinet.

STATS

- Nearly 50 percent of online daters are between the ages of eighteen and thirty-four and about 25 percent of them are between the ages of thirty-five and forty-four.[189]
- Twenty to forty million Americans have used online dating services.[190]
- The bad news for women is that there are only eighty-six unmarried men for every one hundred unmarried women in the United States.[191]

- Idaho and Utah have the most state residents who are married. New York and Washington have the least.[192]

ASSIGNMENTS

First Base: Send your wife a flirty text.

Second Base: Leave her a little note some place where she'll find it and be pleasantly surprised.

Third Base: Write her a long letter with an original poem.

Home Run: Make or buy a cute box where she can put all of your love letters and cards. Tell her she's going to need a big one because it will take that much space for her to store how much you love her.

A LEAGUE OF THEIR OWN

Just because guys don't hang on to every note you ever write doesn't mean you shouldn't put pen to paper and express your love and admiration. They hold on to more things than you think. To fend off flirty female coworkers, provide him with a picture of the two of you that he can keep on his desk, in his locker, or in his workspace. Put something that reminds him of you in his car. Squirt your perfume on something that will make him crazy thinking about you during the day.

Keep everything in perspective by remembering that you're not going to take any of your stuff into heaven with you when you die. The things that truly matter can't be put into a box anyway: relationships, memories, love, testimony, and Christlike qualities you develop over a lifetime.

Chapter 33

THE PITCHER

HONORING YOUR PRIESTHOOD

You will have burdens placed upon you in this life simply because you're a man. You are to be the provider and protector in your family. Those are big responsibilities. Juggling all of the demands of work, home, Church, and everything else will be frustrating, unless you allow the Lord and your wife to help you. Your wife and your children will look to you for priesthood leadership. You won't have time to quickly repent and suddenly make yourself worthy when someone needs a priesthood blessing. Be ready all of the time.

Your priesthood gives you great power. Use your priesthood power wisely and carefully. It is a power to *serve*. It is the same power Jesus Christ used to heal the sick, raise the dead, and create this world. It is predicated upon your faithfulness. In other words, if you don't work, it won't either. Work to be valiant and true at all times.

The priesthood gives you opportunities to lead, serve, and bless others. The priesthood is the power of God given to man on earth

to bless His children. Every time you go home teaching, bless the sacrament, help someone move into a new house, perform ordinances, or any other quorum assignment, you are showing the Lord that He can count on you. A good woman wants to know she can count on you too. She's betting her future and even her eternity on you.

Most LDS women want a worthy priesthood holder in their home to bless their lives and family. Be that man. She will support and honor you. Do not disappoint her or the Lord. They are both counting on you.

In a talk given by President David O. McKay in June of 1965, he outlined the order in which the priesthood brethren will be asked by Jesus Christ to give an accounting of their stewardships:

- An accounting of your relationship with your spouse.
- An individual account of relationships with each child.

- The development of personal talents.
- The fulfillment of Church assignments.
- How honest you were with your dealings.
- An accounting of our contributions to the community.[195]

You may have noticed that there is no "Coach Cooper" in the married section of the book. Instead, I have asked many women what they wanted husbands to know. One of the topics that kept coming up was the lack of priesthood leadership within the home. Yes, they were proud of their husbands for magnifying their callings at church, but when it came to taking the lead on family home evening or nightly prayer, their husbands often waited for the wife to do it. Commit to truly leading your family into heaven. You be the one to gather the kids for daily scripture study or nightly prayer. Your wife *wants* you to be the priesthood leader in your home. She wants to know you take your relationship with her and with God seriously. Lead and she will eagerly follow and support you.

Several years ago, one of my son's priesthood leaders put those big paper clamps on all of the boys' scriptures. They wondered why he was being so weird until he explained the acronym:

C = Commitment to the commandments
L = Listen and learn from the Spirit
A = Act like the priesthood holder you are
M = Mission preparation begins today
P = Pray until you get an answer
S = Study the scriptures instead of just reading them

You might like the idea of putting actual clamps on everything to remind you to prepare your body and spirit every day to be used by the Lord to do His work.

STATS

- More than three-fourths of men in a 2013 study reported feeling guilty about taking a woman's money when she offers to chip in for a date. However, half of women think the man should pay if his income is higher, and only one-third think they should pay if her income is higher.[196]
- While European chivalry has its roots in feudalism in France and Spain, some scholars believe it is nothing more than the continuation of *al-furusiyya al-arabia,* or Arabian chivalry, which was imported to Europe during the early Crusades. The knight-errantry, the riding on horseback to find adventure, the rescue of a maiden in need, the nobility of women, and the connection of honorable conduct with the horse rider are all traceable to Arabia.[197]

- Reaching its highest development in Europe during the twelfth and thirteenth century, chivalry represents a fusion of Christianity and military concepts of the early medieval warrior class. It encompasses ideas of morality, religion, and social codes, such as courage, honor, and service.[198]
- Happy couples have five positive interactions for every negative one.[199]

ASSIGNMENTS

First Base: Study the oath and covenant of the priesthood in Doctrine and Covenants 84.

Second Base: Write down a list of ways the priesthood can bless your sweetheart's life. When you are tempted to not live up to your priesthood covenants, read that list again.

Third Base: Attend the temple regularly with your sweetheart. You will both gain a better understanding of your divine nature.

Home Run: Offer to give your sweetheart or child a priesthood blessing.

A LEAGUE OF THEIR OWN

Let your man be a leader. He may not take the lead on family home evening like you would like him to, but you can nurture that talent in him. Remind him that your children need to see how a valiant priesthood holder acts. Women should be nurturers, not naggers. Women have historically been the ones who are expected to bring refinement and culture to society. Your talents are what will soften a home and convert it from a wild bachelor pad into a nurturing refuge for your family. The family proclamation declares that you are equal with your husband.[200] You don't have to earn the same amount of money in a career outside the home to be of equal value. Your divinely distinct responsibilities have been designated by a loving Heavenly Father who knows your innate qualities and gifts.

Do you remember the part in the Book of Mormon that talks about the valiant stripling warriors and how they praised their mothers for having such strong faith? They credited their success in battle to the teachings of their mothers (see Alma 56). What a wonderful tribute.

By the way, have you ever wondered where the dads of the stripling warriors were during that time? They were actually away from the village, getting provisions. It was a time of war and the men had been called away to get provisions (Alma 56:27). What would you do if your husband had to leave you and your children for a time and you were left alone to take care of everything at home? Do you know how to change an air filter? Can you rewire a broken toaster? Can you change a flat tire? Do you know when to plant seeds for a summer vegetable garden? Develop some of those skills so that you can be capable of running a household with or without a man.

Chapter 34

COMMENTATOR

IMPROVING COMMUNICATION

As the saying goes, men are from Mars and women are from Venus. In other words, men and women think, behave, and communicate differently. A woman wants to know what's going on inside the head of the man she loves. Please don't come home and plop yourself in front of the TV without first connecting with your loved one. Please don't disappear into your cell phone at breakfast without first acknowledging her existence and asking what she has planned for the day. Women need to talk. Women love to talk.

You can learn a lot about a woman by what she says. You can also learn a lot about her by what she does *not* say. Pay attention. If she's angry about something and you're confused about what role you're supposed to play in the situation, simply ask her if she's just venting or if she wants you to help solve a problem. Nine out of ten times, she's just venting. She *has* to talk.

One thing men don't understand about women is that talking is a journey, not a destination. You might ask her a simple question, such as, "Did you have time to get the oil changed in the car today?" You won't get a simple answer. You will hear all about her day, where she went, what the waiting room in the service shop looked like, and what kind of conversation she had with the man sitting next to her. Don't get impatient. You will get the answer to your question eventually. She just has to relive the experience, comment on it, and have you participate in the experience so that you truly understand the answer. Enjoy the journey. Yelling at her for taking so long to answer the question is going to hurt her feelings and send her the message that you don't care. Yeah, maybe you don't care about the conversation she had with someone in the shop while getting the oil changed. That's okay. Just be careful that she doesn't get the impression that you don't care about her and her emotional experiences throughout the day.

So, what's a guy in a hurry to do? What if you don't want to hear every detail of every moment of her day? Hold her hands in a loving way with a smile on your face and say something like, "Honey, I want to hear all about your day, but right now I just need a yes or no answer from you quickly. Later, we can talk more." That's it. You're off the hook. Well, maybe not entirely. If she's tired later, then you might be off the hook and you won't hear about all of the details. If not, be prepared to listen. It will be evidence to her that you keep your word.

Another strategy is to tell her that you don't have time right now to hear all about her day's adventures, but that you'd love to talk in more depth later when you're washing the dishes or folding the laundry together. That will give her something to look forward to.

When life gets super busy and you're not going to be together for several days or more, assure her that you want to hear about everything and encourage her to keep a journal or notes of the highlights that she can share with you later. You'll need to follow up and actually act like you're interested in all of the details, but what usually happens is that the long list will build up and she'll realize she needs to condense it down to the most important things. You save twenty minutes of talking.

Now, if you have a really gabby gal, you may need to simply compromise. Of course, you were probably attracted to her chatty, bubbly personality in the beginning, so you can't say you weren't warned. You can be honest with her and admit that you max out emotionally after thirty minutes or so. Ask her to condense the most important things into whatever time frame you can handle. Find a time limit that allows you both to compromise a little.

There comes a time in marriage when discussing all of the business of the day takes precedence over philosophizing about the meaning of life or other deep subjects. Potty training, the children's grades, your child's rotten baseball coach, and all of those things need to be discussed. Some married couples make a rule that they won't talk about those things during date night so that it's a special time when you just dream together and feed each other's souls. Otherwise, you feel like little more than roommates.

Your wife probably knows that you love her, but she still needs to hear those three magical words often, and I'm not talking about once a year. Yes, your actions also tell her how you feel about her, but I'm telling you now, those words are important. The more you say it, the easier it will be.

When your wife comes to you with a problem, she may or may not want you to actually solve the problem for her. She may already know what she's going to do; she just needs to hear herself say it aloud. Maybe she just needs to vent. She wants to feel understood. She wants her feelings validated. You'll be surprised at how a loving arm around her waist and an "I'm so sorry that you had to go through that" can heal wounds both large and small.

Even the best players need a good coach. Find someone whom you admire who also has a good marriage and ask what he or she does to communicate well. Read books about marriage and relationships. There's also nothing wrong with going to a marriage counselor. I know some couples who go to one without big problems, just for an annual "tune up." In your heart-to-heart talks, address any resentments early on when they are small, long before they explode beyond repair into divorce. Be honest with each other, but always be kind.

Finally, call her! Let her know you're thinking of her. Women eat that stuff up. Be sure to leave out the ulterior motives for the call such as, "Can you get that phone number for me?" or, "Can you pick up my dry cleaning?" Including those kinds of things changes the phone call from a romantic one into a business one. She needs to believe you were just simply thinking of her and wanted to hear her beautiful voice. I love it when my husband calls to tell me he's on his way home and wants to know if I need anything picked up from the store on his way. I rarely need him to run any errands, but he sure scores big points just for asking.

And yeah, you're on the point system. Everything has a point value and your girl is keeping score, even if she doesn't realize it. Don't be mistaken, some things are worth more points than other

things. Just like in baseball, you could score a single, double, or triple. For example, one considerate phone call from you can do much to turn up the thermostat and make it warm and cozy when you arrive home. If you're running late, call her. I'm talking common courtesy here. Most of you have a cell phone, so there is simply no excuse not to call, at least no excuse she can think of that will get you off of the bench you'll be on if you don't let her know. She'll sit and wait up to fifteen minutes for you, telling herself there must be traffic but that you're certainly on your way. After twenty minutes, she will be experiencing a mixture of concern for your safety and annoyance that you haven't kept your word. After thirty minutes, she will be suffering a combination of living her worst nightmares of you dead on the road due to a car crash and being furious at what an unthoughtful beast you are to do this to her. Her worried mind will be busy concocting all sorts of scenarios, and believe me, you don't want her mind racing like this. You will pay dearly for making her stress like this. Just avoid the whole thing by taking two minutes to call her and let her know where you are and how you're progressing. Anticipation can do wonders to spark a flame.

Unfortunately, this whole phone call matter also has to do with trust. If you're always late or you don't call, she's going to start wondering what's really going on. Her concerned mind will start to imagine all kinds of terrible scenarios. Can you be trusted? Is there someone else? A flood of other occasions when your integrity came into question will begin to whirl in her mind.

Some women remember everything; every time you didn't measure up might get recorded on her giant mental checklist. I know; it's not fair. It's just how women's minds work. I'm giving you the heads up here. A simple phone call will only cost a few seconds but earn both of you peace of mind.

I asked Deirdra Eden, a fantastic LDS author, to share her thoughts on marriage and this is what she said: "Open communication in marriage isn't about doing a lot of talking. It's about being completely transparent, vulnerable, trusting, and humble. Marriage requires sacrifice, and not just sacrifice of time or material possessions. It requires that we give up pride, to be more humble; fear, to be more faithful; prejudices, to be more loving; and pain, to be more forgiving."

STATS

- Worldwide, men have a life expectancy of 64.52 years, as compared to a life expectancy of 68.76 years for women, according to the Harvard Medical School.[203]
- Boys are approximately three times more likely to be diagnosed with attention deficit disorder (ADD) or attention deficit and hyperactivity disorder (ADHD) than girls are.[204]
- According to a recent study by David Barash and Judith Eve Lipton, men are nearly three times more likely than women to

abuse alcohol and twice as likely to abuse recreational drugs like marijuana.[205]

ASSIGNMENTS

First Base: When she starts talking, listen.

Second Base: Ask her how her day went. Listen. Be interested. Ask questions. Listen some more. Don't yawn.

Third Base: Listen to her while you're doing the dishes or laundry with her. This is a like hitting a double.

Home Run: Take her out and tell her the evening is all about her. Tell her you want to hear everything. Listen, ask questions, and don't just act interested, be interested.

A LEAGUE OF THEIR OWN

Give the poor guy a break. He loves you, but he's exhausted and doesn't have to hear every thought that crossed your mind during the day. If his eyes are starting to roll back into his head during one of your long monologues, try to condense it all into one or two simple points. Let him know if you need him to act on the information you just gave him or if you just needed him to listen. Thank him for listening!

Chapter 35

YOU'RE OUT!

AVOIDING DIVORCE

So what if your family isn't picture perfect? Join the club. My parents were divorced when I was in elementary school. I remember when the fighting started, and I knew that everything was very wrong. My dad put a wishbone from our Thanksgiving turkey inside a picture frame with a sign that said, "Our family's wish is to stay together." I'll never forget their biggest fight that resulted in a slammed door and the picture crashing to the ground from the shaking wall. I knew it was over at that moment.

Years later, I asked my mother about the divorce. She thought for a moment and said, "I thought getting a divorce would end the problems. It only changed them."

There is no "perfect" family. Every family has challenges and unique struggles. If there is a perfect family, then it's the one that pulls together in tough times and never gives up on one another. But even good people sometimes can't get along. Life is a test. We didn't come here to kick back and play with puppies while drinking soda on the beach. We came here to learn, grow, and stretch.

You get two chances for a happy family in this life: the one you were born with and the one you create when you're married. If the first one wasn't great, then decide now to make the second one fantastic. Identify what *is* good about it and then build on that. Even better, do what you can *now* to improve your family life today, so you'll never get to the point when you think that it's better to leave it than work on it.

Write down

- What works in your family.
- What doesn't work in your family.
- What you can do to improve the environment in your home.
- How you can show love better.

Becoming like Christ is a process, not an event. The commandments do not say, "Be ye therefore perfect by this afternoon." Below is a short list of what you can do to achieve deeper intimacy in your marriage:

- Serve one another. I put this one first because it is the most important thing you can do to protect and heal your marriage. Truly magical words are, "Is there anything I can do for you?"
- Be committed to your marriage. Sure, your spouse isn't the same person you married. Neither are you. Did you really think nothing would change during a lifetime of experiences and challenges? Be the last person to give up on your marriage (unless you are being abused or hurt by your spouse).
- Avoid hurting each other in any way. You know how to push each other's buttons. Stop falling into old patterns by developing some healthier habits.
- Be honest with each other, but always be kind.
- Make yourself the best person you can be so that your spouse will want to be with you.

- Allow yourself to be vulnerable so you can get close to each other.
- Be positive. Believe your marriage can get better.
- Compliment your spouse. Kindness is the consistent base hit that will win the day.
- Attend the temple and keep your covenants.
- Live the gospel and use the Atonement to heal your marriage.
- Let go of the little things that don't matter.
- Make a list of all the reasons why you should stay together. Why is your marriage worth saving? Read this list on a regular basis and make a game plan of how you can do all of the things identified above.

Everyone wants to matter. If you come home from work after being gone for hours and head straight to the pile of mail or the refrigerator and the couch, she's going to think, "He hasn't seen me in hours and those things are more important than me?" Before you do *anything,* head straight to her arms and let her know you're glad to see her.

The number one reason married couples fight is money. The problem is often when one spouse is a saver and one is a spender. Couples need to work together on creating a realistic budget and committing to long-term financial goals they both agree upon. Some wives expect their husbands to be in charge of the finances, but your wife needs to know what's going on too. I've known too many wives who were completely unprepared and uninformed when their husbands suddenly died. Sit down together and conquer your finances before they conquer you. Money is not the most important thing in the world, but it touches everything that is.

Most couples admit that there are certain things in a marriage that would warrant a divorce, such as infidelity, violence, and addictions; however, I also know some couples who have successfully conquered those serious challenges. The Atonement was given to us as a gift to be used on a daily basis. Its healing power is infinite and eternal. It was performed out of love by a perfect Savior, so it certainly can repair any wounded love found in an imperfect marriage.

I used to think that the Atonement was really meant for people who committed terrible sins so that they could repent and try again. I wasn't planning on robbing any banks or killing anyone, so I didn't fully grasp the depth of what the Savior had done for me. It wasn't until I was a young mother that I finally appreciated the part of the Atonement that applied directly to me.

I had just lost my first baby, and my heart was broken. Both my spirit and body grieved for the loss of my little one. I could hardly function and spent days in a dark depression. My husband was hurting too and didn't know how to help me heal. One afternoon, while I was listening to a Church talk to try to calm my tormented soul, I felt the Savior's loving arms embrace me. I knew He was right there next to me. I felt an overwhelming sense of love and peace. I knew that everything would be okay and that the Savior knew me, loved me, and was sad with me. The cleansing tears began to flow down my cheeks. It changed everything for me.

I suddenly remembered that part of the Atonement included the pains of the world Jesus experienced in the Garden of Gethsemane, which were so great that He bled from every pore. He suffered for all of our sins, but He also felt the weight of our troubles and sorrow from mortality, even those not connected with sin. He understood fully what it feels like to be mortal. I realized that Jesus knew exactly how I was feeling because He had felt it already before me. His Atonement washes over sins and the sorrows of mortal living. For the first time, the Atonement became real to me. I knew He could heal my heart and make my burden light. He was the only one who could do it.

I immediately had greater empathy and understanding for others who had lost their babies too. I loved the children I did have even more. I wanted to be better. My trial seemed to shorten the distance between me and my Heavenly Father. I became instantly focused on what truly mattered in life. Would I wish that pain on anyone? Absolutely not, but I recognize the importance of the trial in teaching me some important lessons in life. Sorrow and pain are just a part of this mortal life. The Atonement can wash away our tears and give us hope again. Resolve to get rid of any problems or sins that separate you from God. The Atonement can heal you from those things.

There is a big difference between repenting and feeling bad for mistakes we've made, and just feeling bad because we got caught. There is also a difference between feeling sorrow for our sins and feeling true, godly sorrow when we know we have hurt Heavenly Father because of our disobedience. When we sin, we're simply removing ourselves farther away from God. He's not the one who moved away. We are. Godly sorrow is when we recognize the pain we've caused Him because of our choice to move away from Him.

There is a story about Leonardo da Vinci that illustrates the role we play in our ability to receive inspiration and guidance from

God. Some children were visiting the famous artist one day when one of them accidentally knocked over a stack of canvases. This upset the master artist because he had been working very quietly and sensitively. He instantly became angry, threw his brush on the floor and hurled some harsh words to the frightened little boy, who ran crying from the studio. Leonardo was now alone again, and he tried to continue his work. He was trying to paint the face of Jesus, but he couldn't do it. His creativity had stopped.

Leonardo da Vinci put down his brush and went out into the streets and alleys until he found the little boy. He said "I'm sorry, little one. I shouldn't have spoken so harshly. Forgive me, even as Christ forgives. I have done something far worse than you. You only knocked over the canvases, but I, in my anger, blocked the flow of God into my life. Will you come back with me?" He took the boy back into the studio with him. They smiled as the face of Jesus came quite naturally from the master's brush. That face has been an inspiration to millions ever since.[207]

Focusing on others steadily bathes us with inspiration, motivation, and perspective. Whenever we are going through trials or feeling distanced from Heavenly Father, one of the best things we can do to get an eternal perspective is to serve. Happiness lies within us as we reach out to what is outside of us. Happiness is not what you get but what you give.

STATS

- On average, most men lie twice as often as women.[208]
- The youngest girl to ever be divorced was ten years old.[209]
- Four out of ten workplace dating relationships result in marriage.[210]

ASSIGNMENTS

First Base: Say you're sorry. Whether you think you're right or wrong, a sincere apology is always a good way to mend wounds.

Second Base: Serve her more. Show her more Christlike love.

Third Base: Study the scriptures together more. Pray together more. Attend the temple together more. Reach out to the bishop or a marriage counselor for additional strength and guidance.

Home Run: Repent. Forgive each other. Seek the miracle of the Atonement in your marriage.

A LEAGUE OF THEIR OWN

A man falls in love with a woman in part because of the way he feels about himself when he's with her. When she stops making him feel special, he'll look for someone or something else that will. That's what an affair is all about. That's when addictions begin. Trouble in a relationship begins with three things:

- No talking
- No touching
- No time

Are you doing your part? When you were married, especially if you were sealed in a temple, you promised the Lord you were going to give everything to this new marriage. Have you?

CLOSING THOUGHTS

A loving relationship between a husband and wife is what ties our families together and gives meaning to our lives. Marriage is ordained of God. A wise Father in Heaven designed a plan of happiness where we would get to have a companion to go through mortality with and who would love us even if we stumbled on the path at times during our earthly journey. He wanted us to find a safe place in the loving arms of someone who would cherish, inspire, and help us to be a little better each day. He designed marriage to be a school where we could practice being Christlike with someone who would still love us on the days we don't feel that way. Heavenly Father created marriage to be a refuge from the storms that would most certainly come in our lives. And finally, He wanted us to have joy in this life, and He knew that it would be the most fun to experience this entire adventure with a best friend.

How wonderful it is to have the opportunity of marriage in this life. Like all things worthwhile, it requires work, sacrifice, and the best we have to offer. May your marriage be filled with kindness, passion, laughter, unconditional love, and a lifetime filled with wonder!

NOTES

1. "Tim Salmon Stats," Baseball Almanac, accessed February 2, 2015, http://www.baseball-almanac.com/players/player.php?p=salmoti01.
2. Wayne Stewart, *The Gigantic Book of Baseball Quotations* (New York: Skyhorse Publishing, Inc., 2007), 621.
3. "Ted Williams Quotes," *BrainyQuote*, accessed February 2, 2015, http://www.brainyquote.com/quotes/quotes/t/tedwilliam100519.html.
4. "Birthday Wishes to a Friend of Cooperstown," Tim Wiles, *Cooperstown Chatter*, accessed February 2, 2015, http://baseballhall.mlblogs.com/2011/11/30/birthday-wishes-to-a-friend-of-cooperstown/.
5. "Albert Einstein quotes," *Quote Wise*, accessed February 2, 2015, http://www.quotewise.com/quotes/albert-einstein/you-teach-me-baseball-and-ill-teach-you-relat.
6. "Everything You Wanted to Know About Dating But Were Too Afraid to Ask," popupspeeddating.com, accessed February 5, 2015, http://popupspeeddating.com/everything-about-dating/.
7. Ibid.
8. Ibid.
9. Christina Farr, "Online daters, be warned! 1 in 10 profiles are scams, report reveals," created October 30, 2012, accessed February 5, 2015, http://venturebeat.com/2012/10/30/online-dating-scam/.
10. "Bill Lee Quotes," *BrainyQuote*, accessed February 2, 2015, http://www.brainyquote.com/quotes/quotes/b/billlee139682.html.
11. "Some Good Quotes," Inter County Baseball Association, accessed February 2, 2015, http://www.leaguelineup.com/miscinfo.asp?menuid=33&url=intercountybaseballassociation&sid=1075407.
12. Steve Santagati. *The MANual*.(New York, NY: Crown Publishing, 2007).
13. Lew Jetton, "Strange But True Facts About Men, Women, and Relationships," AM 860, accessed February 5, 2015, http://kpam.com/page.php?page_id=114.
14. Ibid.
15. Ibid.
16. Ibid.
17. "George Brett Quotes," *Baseball Almanac*, accessed February 5, 2015, http://www.baseball-almanac.com/quotes/quobrett.shtml.
18. "The Family: A Proclamation to the World," *Ensign*, November 1995, 102.
19. Spencer W. Kimball, "Oneness in Marriage," *Ensign*, March 1977, accessed February 5, 2015, https://www.lds.org/ensign/1977/03/oneness-in-marriage?lang=eng.
20. Thomas F. Coleman, "Celebrating Our Singularity: The History of Unmarried and Single Americans Week," UnmarriedAmerica.org, accessed February 5, 2015, http://www.unmarriedamerica.org/Celebrating%20Our%20Singularity.pdf.
21. "Facts for Features: Unmarried and Single Americans Week." CensusBureau.gov.

July 21, 2009. Accessed: December 24, 2009, http://www.census.gov/newsroom/facts-for-features/2014/cb14-ff21.html.

22. Dhanika, "Looking for a Date: 7 Types of Dating," *Consumer Instinct*, posted June 18, 2012, accessed February 5, 2015, http://www.consumerinstinct.com/looking-for-a-date-7-types-of-dating/#prettyPhoto.
23. "76 Interesting Facts About . . . Dating and Relationships," Random Facts, accessed February 5, 2015, http://facts.randomhistory.com/dating-and-relationship-facts.html.
24. "Famous Quotes about Dedication," *Book of Famous Quotes*, accessed February 2, 2015, http://www.famous-quotes.com/topic.php?tid=304.
25. Hugh Rawson, Ed., *The Oxford Dictionary of American Quotations* (Oxford: Oxford University Press, 2006), 513.
26. "Search or find what you thought was lost," Baseball Quote of the Day, accessed February 5, 2015, http://quote.webcircle.com/cgi-bin/search.cgi?position=OF%20-%20IF.
27. "Hank Aaron," African American Quotes, accessed February 2, 2015, http://www.africanamericanquotes.org/hank-aaron.html.
28. "51% percent of single people . . ." GrabStats.com, accessed February 5, 2015, http://www.grabstats.com/statmain.aspx?StatID=1380.
29. "63% of married couples . . ." GrabStats.com, accessed February 5, 2015, http://www.grabstats.com/statmain.aspx?StatID=1390.
30. "General," *Sports-Quotes.com*, accessed February 2, 2015, http://www.sports-quotes.com/baseball/general.html.
31. Thomas Nelson, *From a Friend's Heart: 50 Reflections on Living Well*, (Thomas Nelson, Inc., 2006).
32. "How Women Test Men—And you'd better pass!" Expert Men's Dating Advice, accessed February 6, 2015, http://expertmensdatingadvice.com/how-women-test-men-and-youd-better-pass/.
33. Ibid.
34. "76 Interesting Facts About . . . Dating and Relationships," Random Facts, accessed February 6, 2015, http://facts.randomhistory.com/dating-and-relationship-facts.html.
35. Ibid.
36. Ibid.
37. Barney Corkhill, "20 Great Quotes from . . . Baseball: Yogi Berra Special!!" Bleacher Report, created September 16, 2008, accessed February 3, 2015, http://bleacher-report.com/articles/58227-20-great-quotes-frombaseball-yogi-berra-special.
38. David P. Nystrom, *The NIV Application Commentary* (Nashville, TN: Zondervan, 1997), 67.
39. "The Body Baldness Trend," Belgravia Centre, accessed February 6, 2015, http://www.belgraviacentre.com/blog/the-body-baldness-trend-215/.
40. "76 Interesting Facts About . . . Dating and Relationships," Random Facts, accessed February 6, 2015, http://facts.randomhistory.com/dating-and-relationship-facts.html.
41. "93 Revealing Facts About . . . Body Language," Random Facts, accessed February

6, 2015, http://facts.randomhistory.com/body-language-facts.html.
42. Ibid.
43. Ibid.
44. "Strange But True Facts About Men, Women and Relationships!" AM 860, accessed February 6, 2015, http://kpam.com/page.php?page_id=114.
45. "What is Depression?" National Institute of Mental Health, accessed February 6, 2015, http://www.nimh.nih.gov/health/topics/depression/index.shtml.
46. "25 Funny Baseball Quotes," *Huffington Post*, updated December 30, 2012, accessed February 6, 2015, http://www.huffingtonpost.com/david-macaray/baseball-quotes_b_2031178.html.
47. "Dating/Relationship Statistics," Statistic Brain, accessed February 20, 2015, http://www.statisticbrain.com/dating-relationship-stats/.
48. Ibid.
49. Ibid.
50. "On average, there are 86 single men . . ." *GrabStats*, accessed February 10, 2015, http://www.grabstats.com/statmain.aspx?StatID=1376.
51. Eldon L. Ham, *All the Babe's Men: Baseball's Greatest Home Run Seasons and How They Changed America* (Dulles, VA: Potomac Books, 2013), 80.
52. "Brother Randal L. Ridd: 'The choice generation'," *Deseret News*, published April 5, 2014, accessed February 10, 2015, http://www.deseretnews.com/article/865600325/Brother-Randall-L-Ridd-The-choice-generation.html?pg=all.
53. "39 Fun Facts About . . . Flirting," Random Facts, accessed February 10, 2015, http://facts.randomhistory.com/flirting-facts.html.
54. Lisa Wade, PhD, "From Manly to Sexy: The History of the High Heel," *The Society Pages*, created February 5, 2013, accessed February 10, 2015, http://thesocietypages.org/socimages/2013/02/05/from-manly-to-sexy-the-history-of-the-high-heel/.
55. John Willoughby, "Matters of Taste," *The Chicago Tribune*, created February 22, 1995, accessed February 10, 2015, http://articles.chicagotribune.com/1995-02-22/entertainment/9502220240_1_taste-buds-supertasters-linda-bartoshuk.
56. Lorna Collier, "Why We Cry," *American Psychological Association*, published February 2014, accessed February 10, 2015, http://www.apa.org/monitor/2014/02/cry.aspx.
57. "A League of Their Own," *Wikiquote*, accessed February 10, 2015, http://en.wikiquote.org/wiki/A_League_of_Their_Own.
58. "Artificial Grass," *Greenfields*, accessed February 10, 2015, http://www.greenfields.eu/artificial-grass/.
59. "Victor Borge > Quotes," Good Reads, accessed February 10, 2015, https://www.goodreads.com/author/quotes/17226.Victor_Borge.
60. "Ha! Laughing is good for you!" Canada.com, accessed February 10, 2015, http://bodyandhealth.canada.com/channel_section_details.asp?text_id=4982&channel_id=11&relation_id=26288.
61. *Who Framed Roger Rabbit*, directed by Robert Zemeckis (1988; Touchstone Pictures), DVD.
62. "Johann Wolfgang von Goethe Quotes," *BrainyQuote*, accessed February 10, 2015,

http://www.brainyquote.com/quotes/authors/j/johann_wolfgang_von_goeth.html.

63. "39 Fun Facts About . . . Flirting," Random Facts, accessed February 10, 2015, http://facts.randomhistory.com/flirting-facts.html.
64. Ibid.
65. "52 Female Signals of Flirting (Her Love Bucket," *The Love Bucket*, accessed February 10, 2015, http://lovebucketblog.com/52-female-signals-of-flirting-her-love-bucket/.
66. "How to Flirt, According to Science," *The Week*, created March 28, 2014, accessed February 10, 2015, http://m.theweek.com/articles/448643/flirt-according-science.
67. "Sports Quotes," lhup.edu, accessed February 10, 2015, https://www.lhup.edu/~dsimanek/sportquo.htm.
68. "Axioms & Advice," peterga.com, accessed February 10, 2015, http://www.peterga.com/baseball/quotes/axioms.htm.
69. "Marriage in South Korea," *Wikipedia*, accessed February 11, 2015, http://en.wikipedia.org/wiki/Marriage_in_South_Korea.
70. "Ten Myths about Cheating Debunked," *Fox News* Magazine, accessed February 11, 2015, http://magazine.foxnews.com/love/10-myths-about-cheating-debunked
71. "Dating Stats You Should Know," match.com, accessed February 11, 2015, Match.com, http://www.match.com/magazine/article/4671/.
72. "The New Interactive Singles Map," jonathansoma.com, accessed February 11, 2015, http://jonathansoma.com/singles/.
73. "Top 50 Baseball Quotes," rbbaseball.org, accessed February 11, 2015, http://www.rbbaseball.org/Page.asp?n=60976.
74. *Cincinnati Gazette*, editorial, 1879; quoted in "Top 50 Baseball Quotes," rbbaseball.org, accessed February 11, 2015, http://www.rbbaseball.org/Page.asp?n=60976.
75. Richard G. Scott, "The Eternal Blessings of Marriage," *Ensign*, May 2011.
76. "It's Complicated: Who Pays on Dates?" NBC News, accessed February 11, 2015, http://www.nbcnews.com/id/23244363/ns/business-personal_finance/t/its-complicated-who-pays-dates/#.VNlwXebF98E.
77. Ibid.
78. "Baseball Quote of the Day," webcircle.com, accessed February 11, 2015, http://quote.webcircle.com/cgi-bin/search.cgi?idPlayer=361.
79. "Bob Gibson Quotes," *Baseball Almanac*, accessed February 11, 2015, http://www.baseball-almanac.com/quotes/bob_gibson_quotes.shtml.
80. "What Men and Women Want in a Mate," *Science Daily*, accessed February 11, 2015, http://www.sciencedaily.com/releases/2007/09/070903204845.htm.
81. Chantal Vella and Len Kravitz, "Gender Differences in Fat Metabolism," University of New Mexico, accessed February 11, 2015, http://www.unm.edu/~lkravitz/Article%20folder/genderdifferences.html.
82. "USA Quick Facts from the US Census," census.gov, accessed February 11, 2015, http://quickfacts.census.gov/qfd/states/00000.html.
83. "Are Men Better Drivers Than Women?" *ABC News*, accessed February 11, 2015, http://abcnews.go.com/Technology/battle-sexes-men-drivers-women-dye-hard-science/story?id=13841063.

84. Walter Hickey, " Here's How Many Messages Men Have to Send to Women on a Dating Site to be Sure of Getting a Response," *Business Insider*, accessed February 11, 2015, http://www.businessinsider.com/online-dating-message-statistics-2013-7#ixzz3RJ6TWe7w.
85. "Quotations about Baseball," *The Quote Garden*, accessed February 11, 2015, http://www.quotegarden.com/baseball.html.
86. "Charlie Lau Quotes," *Baseball Almanac* accessed February 11, 2015, http://www.baseball-almanac.com/quotes/quolau.shtml.
87. "Ten Interesting Facts about Men and Women," *News.am Style*, accessed February 11, 2015, https://style.news.am/eng/news/1792/10-interesting-facts-about-men-and-women.html.
88. Ibid.
89. "Ten Things Every Woman Should Know about a Man's Brain," *Live Science*, accessed February 11, 2015, http://www.livescience.com/14422-10-facts-male-brains.html.
90. "Famous Baseball Quotes," *Spokane Braves Baseball*, accessed February 11, 2015, http://spokanebravesbaseball.weebly.com/baseball-quotes.html.
91. "Yogi Berra," *Wikiquote*, accessed February 11, 2015, http://en.wikiquote.org/wiki/Yogi_Berra.
92. Gordon B. Hinckley, "He Slumbers Not, nor Sleeps," in Conference Report, April 1983, 4–5.
93. Richard G. Scott, "Trust in the Lord," in Conference Report, October 2014.
94. Deborah Tannen, *You Just Don't Understand: Women and Men in Conversation* (New York: Ballantine Books, 1990); quoted from "You Just Don't Understand," *Wikipedia*, accessed February 11, 2015, http://en.wikipedia.org/wiki/You_Just_Don%27t_Understand.
95. Quoted from "We Really Are Wired Differently!" *Creating a Mind Shift*, accessed February 11, 2015, http://www.creatingamindshift.com/tag/genetic/.
96. Ibid.
97. "Will Women Outpace Men in 2156?" *Nature*, accessed February 11, 2015, http://www.nature.com/news/2004/040927/full/news040927-9.html.
98. "Bob Uecker Qutoes," *BrainyQuote*, accessed February 11, 2015, http://www.brainyquote.com/quotes/quotes/b/bobuecker140050.html.
99. "Yogi Berra Quotes," *BrainyQuote*, accessed February 11, 2015, http://www.brainyquote.com/quotes/quotes/y/yogiberra145940.html.
100. "Dating/Relationship Statistics," *Statistic Brain*, accessed February 11, 2015, http://www.statisticbrain.com/dating-relationship-stats/.
101. Ibid.
102. Ibid.
103. Bruce C. Hafen, "Covenant Marriage," *Ensign*, November 1996.
104. "Yogi Berra Quotes," *BrainyQuote*, accessed February 11, 2015, http://www.brainyquote.com/quotes/quotes/y/yogiberra139947.html.
105. "Rogers Hornsby Quotes," *BrainyQuote*, accessed February 11, 2015, http://www.brainyquote.com/quotes/authors/r/rogers_hornsby.html.
106. Jeffrey R. Holland, "We Are All Enlisted," *Ensign*, November 2011.

107. Ryan Cragun, *From One Missionary To Another: The Ins and Outs of Missionary Life* (Lulu, 2004), 88.
108. Jeffrey R. Holland, "Place No More for the Enemy of My Soul," *Ensign*, May 2010.
109. "Dating/Relationship Statistics," *Statistic Brain*, accessed February 11, 2015, http://facts.randomhistory.com/dating-and-relationship-facts.html.
110. "Search: Team: Athletics," webcircle.com, accessed February 11, 2015, http://quote.webcircle.com/cgi-bin/search.cgi?team=Athletics.
111. "Humphrey Bogart Quotes," *BrainyQuote*, accessed February 11, 2015, http://www.brainyquote.com/quotes/quotes/h/humphreybo378264.html.
112. "The Family: A Proclamation to the World, *Ensign*, November 1995, 102.
113. "76 Interesting Facts about Dating and Reltionships," *Random Facts*, accessed February 11, 2015, http://facts.randomhistory.com/dating-and-relationship-facts.html.
114. Ibid.
115. "Baseball Quotes," *BrainyQuote*, accessed February 11, 2015, http://www.brainyquote.com/quotes/keywords/baseball.html.
116. "Hall of Fame Speech—June 12, 1939," *Babe Ruth*, accessed February 11, 2015, http://www.baberuth.com/quotes/.
117. David A. Bednar, "Things as They Really Are," CES Devotional, May 3, 2009, https://www.lds.org/broadcasts/archive/ces-devotionals/2009/01?lang=eng.
118. "Want More Attention Online?" Match.com, accessed February 11, 2015, http://www.match.com/cp.aspx?cpp=/cppp/magazine/article0.html&articleid=4976.
119. Leslie Ann, "Singles Survey is Very Revealing about Dating," WZOZ 103.1, accessed February 11, 2015, http://wzozfm.com/singles-survey-is-very-revealing-about-dating/?trackback=tsmclip.
120. Ibid.
121. Ibid.
122. "Half of Americans Spy On Their Significant Other," *Complex*, accessed February 11, 2015, http://www.complex.com/pop-culture/2014/02/depressing-facts-about-dating-that-will-make-you-ecstatic-youre-single/half-of-americans-spy-on-their-significant-others.
123. "Quotations about Baseball," *Quote Garden*, accessed February 11, 2015, http://www.quotegarden.com/baseball.html.
124. "Richard G. Scott, "The Transforming Power of Faith and Character," *Ensign*, November 2010.
125. "Ten Things Every Woman Should Know About A Man's Brain," Live Science, accessed February 11, 2015, http://www.livescience.com/6327-10-woman-man-brain.html.
126. Ibid.
127. "Women Spend Nearly One Year Deciding What To Wear," *The Telegraph*, accessed February 11, 2015, http://www.telegraph.co.uk/news/uknews/5783991/Women-spend-nearly-one-year-deciding-what-to-wear.html.
128. "Ten Things You May Not Know About Your Heart," *ABC News*, accessed February 11, 2015, http://abcnews.go.com/blogs/health/2012/02/14/10-things-you-may-not-know-about-your-heart/.

129. "Yogi Berra Quotes," *BrainyQuote,* accessed February 11, 2015, http://www.brainyquote.com/quotes/quotes/y/yogiberra621244.html.

130. Peter Handrinos, *The Funniest Baseball Book Ever: The National Pastime's Greatest Quips, Quotations, Characters, Nicknames, and Pranks* (Kansas City, MO: Andrews McMeel, 2010), 47.

131. Jane Haldane, "How to Have a Happy Relationship," *Coast,* accessed February 11, 2015, http://www.thecoast.net.nz/life/health-wellbeing/well-being/jan-haldane-how-to-have-a-happy-relationship/.

132. "Make Valentine's Day a Relationship Milestone," *CoupleStrong,* accessed February 11, 2015, http://www.couplestrong.com/home-2/.

133. "Strange but True Facts about Men, Women, and Relationships," Home Helpers of Lockport, IL, accessed February 11, 2015, https://www.facebook.com/home-helpersswchicago/posts/10152064187682689:0.

134. "76 Interesting Facts about Dating and Relationships," *Random Facts,* accessed February 11, 2015, http://facts.randomhistory.com/dating-and-relationship-facts.html.

135. "Bill Veeck Quotes," *BrainyQuote,* accessed February 11, 2015, http://www.brainyquote.com/quotes/quotes/b/billveeck173993.html.

136. "Casey Stengel Quotes," *BrainyQuote,* accessed February 11, 2015, http://www.brainyquote.com/quotes/authors/c/casey_stengel.html.

137. "Lifestyles, Dating & Romance: A Study of Midlife Singles," for *AARP The Magazine,* accessed February 11, 2015, http://assets.aarp.org/rgcenter/general/singles_1.pdf.

138. "Relationships Over 50," perfectmatch.com, accessed February 10, 2015, http://www.perfectmatch.com/onlinedating/over50/singles-over-50-dating-facts.asp.

139. "Senior Dating Facts," perfectmatch.com, accessed February 10, 2015, http://www.perfectmatch.com/onlinedating/seniors/senior-dating-facts.asp.

140. "Female Mice Delay Reproductive Aging in Males," *Biology of Reproduction,* accessed February 11, 2015, http://www.perfectmatch.com/onlinedating/seniors/senior-dating-facts.asp.

141. "What Research Tells Us about the Most Successful Relationships," *Lifehacker,* accessed February 11, 2015, http://lifehacker.com/what-research-tells-us-about-the-most-successful-relati-1552386916.

142. "Family Relationships in Later Life," StrongerMarriage.org, accessed February 11, 2015, http://strongermarriage.org/htm/married/family-relationships-in-later-life.

143. "10 Ways to Perk Up Your Relationship," *Psychology Today,* accessed February 11, 2015, https://www.psychologytoday.com/articles/200910/10-ways-perk-your-relationship.

144. "Reggie Jackson Quotes," *Baseball Almanac,* accessed February 11, 2015, http://www.baseball-almanac.com/quotes/quojackr.shtml.

145. "Earl Wilson Quotes," *BrainyQuote,* accessed February 11, 2015, http://www.brainyquote.com/quotes/quotes/e/earlwilson384192.html.

146. "76 Interesting Facts about Dating and Relationships," *Random Facts,* accessed February 11, 2015, http://facts.randomhistory.com/dating-and-relationship-facts.html.

147. Ibid.
148. Thomas S. Monson, "Hallmarks of a Happy Home," *Ensign*, November 1988.
149. "Dating Violence," ACADV, accessed February 11, 2015, http://www.acadv.org/dating.html.
150. GrabStats.com, accessed February 11, 2015, http://www.grabstats.com/statmain.aspx?StatID=1390.
151. Ibid.
152. "Favorite Baseball Quotes," *Baseball Zone*, accessed February 11, 2015, http://www.baseballzone.com/baseball-quotes.
153. "Cal Ripken, Jr. Qutoes," *BrainyQuote*, accessed February 11, 2015, http://www.brainyquote.com/quotes/authors/c/cal_ripken_jr.html.
154. "Cell Phones: Why You Can't Hear Me Now," *Discovery News*, accessed February 11, 2015, http://news.discovery.com/human/cell-phone-frequency-111028.htm.
155. "10 Big Differences Between Men's and Women's Brains," *Masters of Healthcare*, accessed February 11, 2015, http://www.mastersofhealthcare.com/blog/2009/10-big-differences-between-mens-and-womens-brains/.
156. "Why Are Women So Hard to Understand? The 8 Big Differences Between Men's and Women's Brains," *Ezine Articles*, accessed February 11, 2015, http://ezinearticles.com/?Why-Are-Women-So-Hard-to-Understand?-The-8-Big-Differences-Between-Mens-and-Womens-Brains&id=6997712.
157. "Mike Schmidt Quotes," *Baseball Almanac*, accessed February 11, 2015, http://www.baseball-almanac.com/quotes/quoschm.shtml.
158. "Talkin' Baseball: Baseball Quotes," *Baseball Vault*, accessed February 11, 2015, http://www.baseball-vault.com/baseball-quotes.shtml.
159. "Online Dating Statistics," *Statistic Brain*, accessed February 11, 2015, http://www.statisticbrain.com/online-dating-statistics/.
160. Ibid.
161. Ibid.
162. Ibid.
163. "Babe Ruth Quotes," *Baseball Almanac*, accessed February 11, 2015, http://www.baseball-almanac.com/quotes/quoruth.shtml.
164. "Juliana Hatfield Quotes," *BrainyQuote*, accessed February 11, 2015, http://www.brainyquote.com/quotes/quotes/j/julianahat328189.html.
165. "Many Don't Wash Hands After Using the Bathroom," *New York Times*, accessed February 11, 2015, http://www.nytimes.com/2005/09/27/health/27wash.html?_r=0.
166. "Barriers to High School Completion Create Barriers to Economic Mobility," *The Heritage Foundation*, accessed February 11, 2015, http://www.heritage.org/research/reports/2014/05/barriers-to-high-school-completion-create-barriers-to-economic-mobility.
167. Richard A Settersten Jr. and Barbara Ray, "What's Going on with Young People Today? The Long and Twisting Path to Adulthood," *Future of Children*, accessed February 11, 2015, http://futureofchildren.org/futureofchildren/publications/docs/20_01_02.pdf.
168. "Baseball Quotes," angelfire.com, accessed February 11, 2015, http://www.angelfire.com/ak2/Studs/quotes.html.

169. Ibid.
170. "Sienna Miller Syndrome: Why a Woman Owns 111 Handbags in Her Lifetime," DailyMail.com, accessed February 11, 2015, http://www.dailymail.co.uk/news/article-478816/Sienna-Miller-syndrome-Why-woman-owns-111-handbags-lifetime.html.
171. "Random Facts," factslides.com, accessed February 11, 2015, http://www.factslides.com/i-477.
172. "Demographics of Russia," *Wikipedia*, accessed February 11, 2015, http://en.wikipedia.org/wiki/Demographics_of_Russia.
173. "How Can a 50 Year Old Woman Lose Weight?" *Live Strong*, accessed February 11, 2015, http://www.livestrong.com/article/398730-how-can-a-50-year-old-woman-lose-weight/.
174. "Does Gender Have an Effect on Hiccups?" *How Stuff Works*, accessed February 11, 2015, http://health.howstuffworks.com/diseases-conditions/respiratory/gender-hiccups.htm.
175. "Search: Position: Manager," webcircle.com, accessed February 11, 2015, http://quote.webcircle.com/cgi-bin/search.cgi?position=Manager&page=11.
176. "Baseball," *Creative Quotations*, accessed February 11, 2015, http://creativequotations.com/tqs/tq-baseball.htm.
177. "Romantic Love Lasts Just One Year," *Complex*, accessed February 11, 2015, http://ca.complex.com/pop-culture/2014/02/depressing-facts-about-dating-that-will-make-you-ecstatic-youre-single/romantic-love-lasts-just-one-year.
178. "The Average Wedding Costs $20,000," *Complex*, accessed February 11, 2015, http://www.complex.com/pop-culture/2014/02/depressing-facts-about-dating-that-will-make-you-ecstatic-youre-single/the-average-wedding-costs-20000.
179. "Couples Only Spend Two Hours a Day Together, Half of Which is Spent Watching TV," *Complex*, accessed February 11, 2015.
180. "Marriage and Divorce Statistics," *Avvo*, accessed February 11, 2015, http://www.avvo.com/legal-guides/ugc/marriage-divorce-statistics.
181. "10 Things Every Woman Should Know About a Man's Brain," *Live Science*, accessed February 11, 2015, http://www.livescience.com/6327-10-woman-man-brain.html.
182. Ibid.
183. "The Not So Greats," peterga.com, accessed February 11, 2015, http://www.peterga.com/baseball/quotes/notgreat.htm.
184. "Dating/Relationship Statistics," *Statistic Brain*, accessed February 11, 2015, http://www.statisticbrain.com/dating-relationship-stats/.
185. "Awkward First Kiss Video and Dating Facts," *SHK*, accessed February 11, 2015, http://seenheardknown.com/lifestyle/awkward-first-kiss-video-dating-facts/.
186. Ibid.
187. "Willie Mays Quotes," *Baseball Almanac*, accessed February 11, 2015, http://www.baseball-almanac.com/quotes/quomays.shtml.
188. "Search: Team: Cardinals," webcircle.com, accessed February 11, 2015, http://quote.webcircle.com/cgi-bin/search.cgi?team=Cardinals.
189. "76 Interesting Facts about Dating and Relationships," *Random Facts*, accessed

February 11, 2015, http://facts.randomhistory.com/dating-and-relationship-facts.html.

190. "Dating Stats You Should Know," Match.com, accessed February 11, 2015, http://www.match.com/magazine/article/4671/.

191. Ibid.

192. Ibid.

193. "Search: Jesse Russell Orosco," webcircle.com, accessed February 11, 2015, http://quote.webcircle.com/cgi-bin/search.cgi?idPlayer=217.

194. George Plimpton, *Out of My League* (Guilford, CT: Lyons Press, 2010), 94.

195. Quoted in Edward D. Smith, "The Things that Matter Most," BYU–Hawaii Devotional, November 2, 2010; access at http://devotional.byuh.edu/script/things-matter-most.

196. "32 Interesting Facts about Chivalry," *Random Facts*, accessed February 11, 2015, http://facts.randomhistory.com/chivalry-facts.html.

197. Ibid.

198. Ibid.

199. Shruti S. Poulsen, "A Fine Balance: The Magic Ratio to a Healthy Relationship," Purdue University, accessed February 11, 2015, https://www.extension.purdue.edu/extmedia/cfs/cfs-744-w.pdf.

200. "The Family: A Proclamation to the World," *Ensign*, November 1995, 102.

201. "Search: Location: Los Angeles," webcircle.com, accessed February 11, 2015, http://quote.webcircle.com/cgi-bin/search.cgi?city=Los%20Angeles&page=3.

202. "Select Category: Information," *Franklin Baseball*, accessed February 11, 2015, http://www.leaguelineup.com/information.asp?url=franklinbaseball&catid=69701.

203. "32 Random Facts about Men," *Random Facts*, accessed February 11, 2015, http://facts.randomhistory.com/2009/06/11_men.html.

204. Aaron Kipnis, *Angry Young Men: How Parents, Teachers, and Counselors Can Help "Bad Boys" Become Good Men* (San Francisco: Jossey-Bass, 2002).

205. "32 Random Facts about Men," *Random Facts*, accessed February 11, 2015, http://facts.randomhistory.com/2009/06/11_men.html.

206. "Hall of Fame Speech—June 12, 1939," *Babe Ruth*, accessed February 11, 2015, http://www.baberuth.com/quotes/.

207. Robert H. Schuller, *The Be Happy Attitudes* (Nashville: Thomas Nelson, 1997).

208. "Men Lie Six Times a Day and Twice as Often as Women, Study Finds," DailyMail.com, accessed February 11, 2015, http://www.dailymail.co.uk/news/article-1213171/Men-lie-times-day-twice-women-study-finds.html.

209. "10 Years Old . . . And Divorced," *New York Post*, accessed February 11, 2015, http://nypost.com/2010/02/14/10-years-old-and-divorced/.

210. "76 Interesting Facts about Dating and Relationships," *Random Facts*, accessed February 11, 2015, http://facts.randomhistory.com/dating-and-relationship-facts.html.

ABOUT *the* AUTHOR

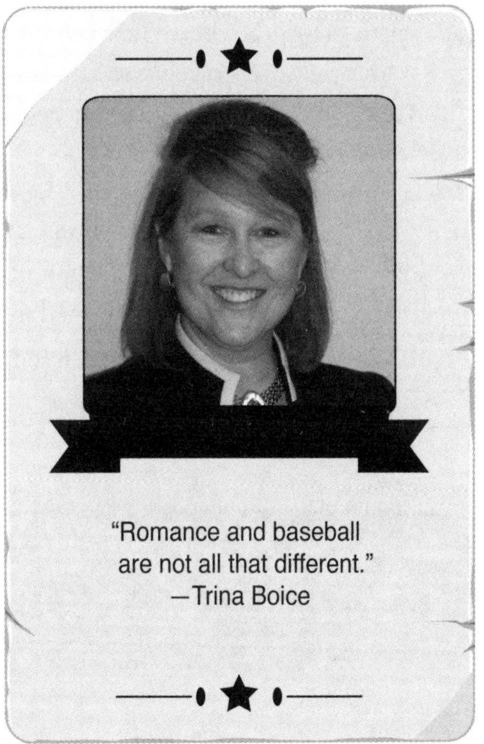

Trina Boice grew up in California, but she currently lives in Las Vegas, Nevada. In 2004 she was honored as the California Young Mother of the Year, an award which completely amuses her four sons. She earned two bachelor's degrees from BYU. She was president of the National Honor Society Phi Eta Sigma and served as ASBYU Secretary of Student Community Services.

Trina also studied at the University of Salamanca in Spain and later returned there to serve an LDS mission in Madrid for a year and a half. She has a real estate license, travel agent license, two master's degrees, and a black belt in Tae Kwon Do, though she's the first to admit that she'd pass out from fright if she were ever really attacked by a bad guy.

She worked as a legislative assistant for a congressman in Washington, DC, and was given the Points of Light Award and Presidential Volunteer Service Award for her domestic and international community service. She wrote a column called "The Boice Box" for a newspaper in Georgia, where she lived for fifteen years.

She currently writes for several websites and is the Entertainment News Editor for Bella Online. Check out her movie reviews at www.MovieReviewMaven.blogspot.com.

Trina was selected by KPBS in San Diego to be a political correspondent during the last presidential election. A popular and entertaining speaker, Trina is the author of twenty-one books, with another one hitting stores soon. You can read more about her books and upcoming events at www.trinaboice.com.

ABOUT *the* CONTRIBUTOR

Cooper served a mission in Argentina and recently graduated from Brigham Young University with a degree in finance. He currently teaches escape and evasion classes in Arizona. Check out his website at www.SpyEscapePhoenix.com.

He trained with Army Special Forces for several years, worked with the National Security Agency, was a gold medalist at the All Army Small Arms Championship, and is currently a Combat Engineer Officer. He enjoys chopping wood, opening pickle jars, and other manly activities, and hopes to be able to grow a beard one day.